The Man who Makes Heads with His Hands

The Art and Life of
Harold Pfeiffer, Sculptor

John A. Stevens and Harold Pfeiffer

Published by

GSPH

General Store Publishing House
1 Main Street, Burnstown, Ontario, Canada K0J 1G0
1-800-465-6072 or Fax: (613) 432-7184

©1997
John A. Stevens
Harold S. Pfeiffer

General Store Publishing House gratefully acknowledges the assistance of the
Canada Council and the Ontario Arts Council.

Canadian Cataloguing in Publication Data

Pfeiffer, Harold, 1908-1997
Stevens, John A. 1949-
        The man who makes heads with his hands:
        the art and life of Harold Pfeiffer, sculptor

ISBN 1-896182-70-4
ISBN 1-896182-67-4 HC

        1.Pfeiffer, Harold, 1908-1997 2. Sculptors--Canada--
Biography, I. Stevens, John A., 1949- II. Title.

NB249.P48A2 1997   730'.92   C97-900210-9

Design: EarthLore Communications
Printed and bound in Canada

Dedication

I would like to dedicate this book to the memory of my late nephew
Reg Pfeiffer, in gratitude for the many flights across Canada in
his plane to the Queen Charlotte Islands, to Nome, Alaska,
and to many remote settlements in the high arctic.
He was a great pilot, and the best critic I ever had.

Harold Pfeiffer

Contents

Introduction

Stuart M. Hodgson CC, former Commissioner of the Northwest Territories

Nowhere on earth are there lands more inhospitable and mysterious than the lands bordering on the polar sea. Much has been written about the early adventurers and explorers and their first encounters with the native inhabitants. They believed the natives were lost in that harsh part of the world; doomed to spend their short time on earth in an ice-covered waste of water and land bordering the polar sea.

The fact is that the inhabitants of this vast area and their ancestors had lived on these lands for thousands of years, never dreaming they were lost. Most had no knowledge, memory or history of the empires, nations and millions of people living to the south. To this day, only a handful of the world's huge population has ever met an arctic native, let alone visited the land northern people call home.

My first encounter with the arctic was during the second world war on the Murmansk run. It was some twenty years before I once again crossed the arctic circle, and even later before I visited most of the countries bordering on the polar sea. I soon realized that these truly magnificent people and their customs, languages, traditions and way of life should be protected and celebrated. One of the many problems was that there was very little exchange among them, though there was little doubt that they were related, having migrated many centuries ago across that forbidding land.

One day, some four years after I returned once more to the arctic, some colleagues from the Northwest Territories Council and I, along with our wives, were on a summer tour of the central arctic. Few of them had ever been to that part of the north in the summer months. It was during that tour that I met one of the most remarkable among the extraordinary individuals that one always seems to meet in the north. Harold Pfeiffer, a sculptor from Ottawa, was hard at work sculpting portrait busts of some native people at Pelly Bay. At that moment he was doing a bust of Theresa Kernak for Calgary's Glenbow Museum.

We didn't have a museum in the NWT at the time. Harold's work was excellent. Here was an artist, no doubt working for peanuts, doing what he could in his own way to preserve a visual history of the Inuit people in their own environment. Right then and there I decided to persuade him to help us record in bronze the people of the arctic. Harold agreed and, as he was at home wherever he worked, he assured me he preferred living with the people in their communities, rather than have them travel to him. We decided he would do six heads a year. The bronze busts would include Inuit, Dené, Métis, former commissioners and members of the NWT Council, bush pilots and others.

As we travelled across the polar sea to other countries, we came to know our neighbours and recognized the similarities among the peoples. It was then that I commissioned Harold as our representative to go to Greenland, Alaska and Lapland, and hopefully one day to Siberia. I was determined to build a museum and heritage centre for the north if it was the last thing I did in the Northwest Territories. Harold Pfeiffer's complete collection of bronze busts of the polar sea people would be preserved there forever.

The northern people owe a great debt to this remarkable man, who kept his end of the bargain. Harold's determination and dedication will be there for people yet unborn to see. HRH the Prince of Wales opened the museum that bears his name on April 3, 1979. It was indeed the last thing I did in the north, as my wife Pearl and I left on the thirteenth of April, thus ending the happiest days of our lives.

There are many people in the world who can copy the work of others; there are only a few who can see what others do not, and create a record of that vision.
Harold Pfeiffer is one of those gifted individuals.

Stuart M. Hodgson, CC

Foreword

As a lawyer's document might say, herewith a series of snippets from a long and semi-adventurous life. For the official introduction, I am indeed grateful. When Stuart Hodgson was the Commissioner of the Northwest Territories, his enthusiasm for my work was of inestimable value.

The continual hounding and encouragement by some of the following are the main reasons for this outpouring: May Willmot, Marg Stevenson Reilley, Norman Fowler, Rolly Murray, Keith Crowe, Keith Arnold, Mary Gleave, Sandra Reilley, Nona Bisset, George Foster and Peg Sullivan. Forgive me if I have left out a few. They kept after me, did much editing "B.C.," before computers. A full chapter could be written about each of them. I must also thank Edwin Lindberg, who very kindly provided us with the story about Albert Faille.

I have always suffered from long-windedness, though I suppose others have done the suffering. As a young person I was frightfully verbose in relating stories about minor adventures to the family and they would interrupt me and say, "OK, start at the third chapter." My middle name starts with S but it does not stand for succinct. Had not my editor intervened, this would have ended up in three volumes.

Artists are another breed. Their perspective of life is something quite unique. In reading this book, I would like the reader to note that I am an unabashed name dropper, a head hunter and a people collector.

Harold Pfeiffer

Preface

Thin, seemingly frail, with a twinkle in his eye that flames when he speaks of his
passion, Harold Pfeiffer sits surrounded by his life's work: hundreds of bronze portraits, dominated
by likenesses of arctic native people, faces deeply marked by their lives as survivors in the wild,
harsh north. In a lifetime of sculpting Harold Pfeiffer has created a unique collection of bronze
portraits of Inuit in Canada, Alaska, Greenland and Siberia, and of native people from Canada's
west. The work is intensely realistic, radiating the powerful presence of great portraiture; vital,
eloquent, real. The intimacy of the portraits is astonishing, preserving in three dimensions the
form and spirit of a vanished people, though they are individuals, not types.

Pfeiffer has been a frequent visitor to the north, though never a resident for long; a stranger
with the strange art of making heads with his hands, taking his likenesses and casting them in
bronze. To date there are ninety-one portraits of aboriginals, which are held in two major collections, one in the Glenbow Museum in Calgary, and the other in the Prince of Wales
Northern Heritage Centre in Yellowknife. His work can also be seen in a number of other public
collections, including the Churchill Museum in Churchill, Manitoba, La Musée d'art in Joliette,
Quebec, the R.C.M.P. Museum in Regina, Saskatchewan and the Museum of Civilization in Hull,
Quebec. A list of private owners of his works constitutes a veritable international Who's Who,
including King Hussein of Jordan, Helmut Kohl, former Chancellor of Germany, Mr. Andreotti,
former Prime Minister of Italy, François Mitterand, former President of France, Sr. Pérez de
Cuéllar, former Secretary General of the UN, and the estate of Henry Moore in England.

The fascination of biography for me is that it provides an opportunity to savour the mystery
of another's life. After hundreds of hours with Harold and his work, I have made many discoveries
and he has recovered many memories. We have not concocted any facile explanations for the
life he has lived and the extraordinary things he has done. We have assembled a narrative that
records that life so that others will know and wonder.

This is the story, and these are the stories, of the Man Who Makes Heads
With His Hands.

John Stevens

Adolphus E. Pfeiffer, Harold's father, ca 1910

Lily Ann Braithwaite Wright Pfeiffer, Harold's mother

Early Years: Quebec City

Harold Samson Pfeiffer was born in 1908 in Quebec City, the youngest of nine in a prosperous Presbyterian family. He was a premature baby and not expected to live. His mother was forty-six and quite ill. These circumstances led Harold's father Adolphus to send for a nanny from Scotland. Annie Michelson looked after him for the first five years of his life.

Harold's was an artistic family; his mother Lily Ann and two of his older brothers, Walter and Gordon, were accomplished painters. As Harold recalls it, his older brothers suggested that three painters in the family were quite enough. They pointed out that Harold was especially good at modelling and suggested he specialise in that. He had taken to modelling at an early age, using clay dug from a bank near the family's summer home at Lac Beauport and firing the work in the fireplace.

The Pfeiffers were second generation German Swiss from Berne. Harold's great uncle Thelo was a child prodigy and not only played the violin but was a violin maker as well. He taught at the Conservatoire de Musique and participated in organising the Quebec Symphony. Sigismund was the maker of the Pfeiffer piano. Records speak of *les trois frères* playing in concerts, referring to Harold's grandfather and his two brothers.

Harold's mother Lily Ann in 1917 at the age of 55, first woman to fly in Quebec City.

The senior Pfeiffer was a successful businessman. He had brought the skills acquired in his family's dyeing business with him, and when Harold's father inherited it, he expanded it with dry cleaning and laundry.

Harold's father was christened Edward Adolphus but changed his names so that he wouldn't have the same initials as his father, who was also E.A.P. He was generally known as Dolph. He had a twin brother, Thomas, who died when he was four. A life-size painting of the two boys rolling hoops was a constant reminder which hung in the Pfeiffers' home for many years.

Harold's father followed a strict Presbyterian regime and never allowed alcohol or card-playing in the house. More peculiarly, cheese was forbidden as well. Harold thinks this is because his grandparents had always kept a wheel of Limburger in the pantry, and its emanations filled his father's childhood home, turning young Adolphus against cheese forever.

"Father was a stern man and a strict father, but he provided a marvellous childhood for all of us. Although I believe he had his doubts about the reality of God from time to time, he was a strict Presbyterian all the same, and intended that all of us should be so, too. Sunday mornings started early; father was up and playing hymns on either the organ or the piano. Then, scrubbed, polished and breakfasted, we were all lined up and checked for clean hankies before we were marched up rue St. Stanislas to church. Here we had a large pew with two upholstered corner benches and a table in the centre for our hymn books, plus footstools for the two youngest to sit on when we had visitors with us."

It seemed to Harold that there were always visitors, and they were expected to accompany the family to church. Having a large house, the Pfeiffers were often called on to put up visiting clergy. The children resented this because of the restraints put on their behaviour. They attended Sunday church services both morning and evening, and Sunday School in the afternoon. Dolph Pfeiffer was an elder and a prominent supporter of St. Andrew's Church. He often declared that a drop of alcohol would never pass his lips; he was so committed about this that he had his wife make non-alcoholic grape juice to substitute for the wine at communion. His antipathy to liquor probably developed during his childhood, as his father was said to have been quite a boozer, a drinking companion of the painter Krieghoff.

Dolph Pfeiffer was a handsome man. He always made sure that his shirts were clean, his suits pressed, and his shoes shined, and he expected the same of his children.

He himself might have been a good artist if he had taken the time for it; after his death a portfolio of very good drawings was found in his desk. He also played the piano and had a great interest in music. With some friends, he started an organization called "Star Course Concerts" through which well-known singers and instrumentalists were brought to Quebec City to perform. Many of them were entertained in the Pfeiffer home.

Dolph developed a passion for automobiles when they arrived on the scene. In 1902, with his great friend Sir George Garneau, he went off to the World's Fair in St. Louis. They were enchanted by the horseless carriages and each bought one.

Much to his delight, Pfeiffer's car arrived three weeks earlier than Sir George's, making him the first man to have a car in Quebec City. He told his children fantastic tales of the awful roads and the many close calls when the behemoth met up with horses and buggies. He remained keen on the newfangled sport of motoring, and continued to attend annual exhibitions in Cleveland and Chicago, buying the latest models. Harold can remember a Stanley Steamer, a McLaughlan-Buick, an Oldsmobile, a Rambler, a Reo, a Dodge, an eight-cylinder and a twelve-cylinder Packard, and a Kurtz automatic.

Harold's mother, Lily Ann Braithwaite Wright, was born in Ballyshannon, Donegal, Ireland. Her father, Francis Edward Wright, was a wheelwright whose ancestors were Scots named MacIntyre. They fought with Bonnie Prince Charlie, and had to flee the country after Cullodon and changed their name to Wright. Her mother was related to the English noble house of Marlborough, and to the same branch of the Wolfe family as General Wolfe, who led the English invasion of Quebec. Wright was a well-established businessman who owned a six-floor flour mill; he moved his family to Cleveland, Ohio when his sons were fifteen and sixteen to give them better opportunities in life. He manufactured wheelbarrows and a two-wheeled hand cart of his own invention which his sons sold in their spare time. One of the boys, Harold's Uncle Samson, founded the Atlas Nut and Bolt Company and the Atlas Car and Manufacturing Company, which made locomotives.

Lily Ann met Adolphus when she was visiting a friend in Quebec City. As a young person in Ireland, she had been a fine horsewoman and brought home many jumping trophies. Her main hobby, though, was painting, especially horses and dogs. Lily Ann was also a talented pianist and was a guest artist at many church concerts and charity affairs.

She was a very spirited woman. During World War I, when the temper of the time was hostile to anything German, including Canadians with German names, the editor of the newspaper wrote a highly prejudicial article about Adolphus Pfeiffer, even though he had been a classmate of Dolph's and knew the family. Lily Ann marched into his office and told him that if he didn't apologize for it in print she would horsewhip him publicly. He immediately printed an apology.

She was also a very religious person. She was originally Church of Ireland, and Episcopalian in the USA, but became a member of Dolph's Presbyterian church on her marriage. She was a great supporter of foreign missions, and the Grenfell Mission was one of her pet projects.

Harold's first exposure to the arctic and its native peoples was through his mother's support of Sir Wilfred Grenfell and his mission among the Labrador Inuit. Starting in the late 1800s and continuing until the 1930s, Grenfell organised and raised funds for hospitals, nursing stations and schools in Labrador. Harold attended a number of Grenfell's lectures with his mother in Quebec, and was inspired by his heroic life.

"Father was very much against foreign missions, as he felt we should help the poor at home instead. They had many arguments about this, but Mother usually got her money for them. My interest in the Inuit was sparked very early by going to Wilfred Grenfell's lectures and meeting him at home. I admired him very much."

The Adolphus Pfeiffer family, ca 1913-14, left to right: Ted, Marjorie, Lily Ann, Adolphus, Walter, Gordon, Harold with dog

Lily Ann developed an interest in aviation when her eldest son, Walter, was a flying instructor in the Royal Canadian Flying Corps during World War I. She was the first woman in Quebec to go up in a plane. She maintained her interest in aviation developments all her life, and amazed people with her knowledge. She was ninety-three when she died, and maintained a strong interest in life until the end. Yet her life could not have been easy. She lost four of her nine children, two at birth and two to childhood diseases. In mid-life she went through the traumatic loss of the family business and then her husband's death.

Harold's earliest memories are of their home on St. Stanislas Street in Upper Town. This was a large home which fronted on the street, with beautiful French windows at the back overlooking a large garden. The house was across the street from Artillery Park and Dominion Arsenal. Built in 1756, the beams in the attic, where the children often played, showed the scars of shell fire from the battles for Quebec, and when Harold's mother began gardening there, several large cannon balls were unearthed on the property.

"Lac Beauport, where father built a summer home, is another of my great early memories. In fact, when I was quite young, I was sent there every winter for a few years to be fattened up by Annie, my former nanny, who had married a farmer who lived nearby."

Summers at Lac Beauport were idyllic. At that time it bore no resemblance to the busy suburb of Quebec City it has become today. There were only seventeen other houses on the whole lake, and the water was clear as crystal. It was easy to catch a good-sized trout any day for breakfast. The summer home's eight bedrooms were almost always full; each of the five children were allowed to have a special friend to visit sometime during the summer. They swam and picnicked, played tennis, boated and climbed the mountain behind the house.

It was here that Harold first discovered his interest in modelling, which led him to sculpture. There was a place on the lakeshore near one of the boat houses where the clay was good for modelling. Harold and his friends spent endless hours making ash trays, Indian heads, pigs, "or whatever else caught our fancy. I still have one of the pigs."

Even at Lac Beauport they weren't allowed to play on Sundays, although they could swim if they didn't make a sport of it. Sunday was the day their mother organised nature walks. They collected as many different species of wild flowers as they could, and looked them up when they returned. Lily Ann would quiz them to see who had learned the most. Or they might collect leaves and find out what trees they came from. Although, at the time, he would rather have been left to play, Harold now recognises that the knowledge and curiosity about nature that these activities encouraged developed his powers of observation and have enriched his life.

"When Mother criticised our art, she would point out little things that we had completely missed, such as the shading of leaves when they curve away from or into light, and the effect light has on the impact of a work of art. It became very important to me, in creating my bronze portraits, to consider the effect of light and shadow on the finished sculpture."

"We received *The Illustrated London News* and frequently there were photographs of well-known stage or screen celebrities or politicians sculpted in bronze." One favourite was the American sculptor Jo Davidson, who worked in France. He made portraits of many prominent people of his day, including Charles Chaplin, Clarence Darrow, Walt Whitman, Franklin D. Roosevelt, Helen Keller and George Bernard Shaw. "His work was quite detailed and I made a habit of cutting out illustrations of his portraits for my album. Other sculptors high on my list were Epstein, Mestrovic, Barlach and Carl Milles.

"The work of the American artist Malvina Hoffman really fascinated me. Maybe it was because she travelled the world in search of unique characters in out-of-the-way places. This whetted my appetite for travel and for doing the same with our Indians and Inuit people."

Harold's great friend when he was twelve or thirteen was Paul Châteauvert, who was a classmate and a neighbour on Grand Allée. Paul died suddenly of spinal meningitis. Shared grief at the loss brought him together with Paul's younger brother Peter. They had tea at Peter's home almost every day after school in the second floor living room, which held a large trestle table where they assembled model planes or laid the tracks of their joint sets of electric trains. Madame Châteauvert was a knowledgeable enthusiast of antiques, and frequently had a friend drop in to discuss the fascinating details of the design of china pieces or Chippendale and Sheraton furniture. This was where Harold's extensive knowledge of antiques was founded.

"When I was taking courses at the Victoria and Albert and at the Louvre, my lecturers were surprised at my knowledge of the details that the great masters used in their designs. Tea break at number 127 Grande Allée was responsible."

Harold's eldest brother, Walter, at the age of twelve, encouraged a few older boys to start a Boy Scout troop in Quebec City in 1908. When Harold was old enough he became active and eventually became a King's Scout. He led boy scout parades on horseback. For many years they had their Scout camp on the mountain behind the Pfeiffer's house at the lake. Harold can recall one occasion when there was a tremendous thunderstorm; the accompanying torrents of water devastated the camp.

"Twenty-three drenched and frightened youngsters poured into our house. Mother gave them lots of hot chocolate and bundled them into blankets while they dried themselves around the fireplace. Finally she tucked them into bed, three in a bed and one on every available couch, to finish out the night."

Describing himself as one of the skinniest boys in Quebec City, and always wearing glasses, Harold didn't like sports, and hated it when he was dragged into team sports like baseball. He did, however, like skiing, which he learned when they lived on Grande Allée, close to the Plains of Abraham. Everyone in Quebec City seemed to learn to ski there.

One of Harold's greatest pleasures when he was a little older was to invite a few friends to Lac Beauport for a skiing weekend. Only the kitchen had a proper foundation; it was the only room which could be kept reasonably warm in winter. They brought in two double beds and, if there was an overflow, there were two maids' bedrooms above the kitchen which could be used. They kept the stove red-hot at night and it was Harold who had to get up every hour to feed more wood into it. On Sunday, more friends would ski down the lake for hot chocolate or a picnic lunch.

Living in the country during World War I was not all beer and skittles. For the duration, Dolph had the large field alongside the house ploughed up and planted in potatoes. Harold remembers spending half the holidays picking bugs or spraying the plants with Paris Green. Much of the work was done by his older brothers and the hired man, but, "Oh how we hated those bloody bugs."

Lily Ann was an ardent gardener and grew all kinds of vegetables and flowers. Harold had his own little wild flower garden where he transplanted such plants as pitcher plant and *calopogans* from the swamps. The latter were unique to the region. Some of his flowers even went to Princess Alice's garden in England. Harold met her when she visited Quebec City and talked with her about his garden. She showed such an interest in it that, when she left Canada, he dug some for her to take with her. She later wrote to say they had been planted and were doing well.

According to the census of 1929, Quebec City was about 75,000 French speaking and 7,500 English speaking, though the anglophones had a great deal of influence. The youthful (and bilingual) Harold was not impressed. "I used to think what a dull bunch of people they were in Quebec City. Those who could afford it went to Florida or Arizona, never venturing to places where customs, language and scenery were completely different. Some of the English speaking families suffered from a *fausse noblesse,* owing their upper-middle-class status to inheritances from their forebears' sometimes-questionable business successes. They seemed to contribute little to the welfare of the community."

Harold Pfeiffer, King's Scout, ca 1922-23

It was a society divided by language and culture, and also by religion. Since Harold spoke French he was able to cross the line. In fact he was actively cultivated as an eligible bachelor by some of the prominent French matrons with daughters of marriageable age. For a time the Pfeiffers lived on de la Tour Avenue, across from Louis St. Laurent, later Prime Minister of Canada. His daughter Marte and Harold used to ride horseback together. When she was in Montreal at a convent school, Harold wrote to her on pale pink paper, using a woman's name and feigning feminine handwriting, since she was strictly forbidden correspondence with a male.

The house on de La Tour evokes other memories:

"The two car garage was too short for the Packard, and Father found it necessary to have it enlarged. When the men dug the foundation, we were horrified to find numerous human skeletons emerging from the earth." In 1847 there had been a cholera epidemic in the city. People died like flies and had to be interred immediately. They were buried in piles in hastily-dug ditches, without coffins.

Harold's eldest brother, Walter, was a medical student at the time, and skeletons were of considerable interest to him. One evening he and Harold went out with a flashlight and gathered up several skulls and bones.

"Strangely, at the time I was not concerned by my ghoulish behaviour. Right after this, I left for a year's study in Europe, and when I returned, I was horrified to find a human skull, complete with teeth, sitting on my dresser!"

Winter in Quebec City at that time was a season of parties, especially during the Christmas and Easter holidays. Formal invitations were sent out three weeks ahead and it was obligatory to reply in writing. Usually the dance or ball was held at a hotel. The less expensive way to entertain was at a tea dance, usually at the Château Frontenac, from four to six o'clock.

For a few years, the Roman Catholic bishop forbade dancing, and many parents of that faith obeyed his edict. However, some Catholics, who were more concerned about their daughters' futures than the bishop's opinion, permitted their daughters to attend tea dances. One could be sure that a young woman's mama and perhaps some of her lady friends were not far away, watchfully sipping tea in the background. Harold frequently attended these parties, as he loved dancing and was a good dancer.

The most elegant party Harold remembers attending was the State Ball held in the parliament buildings in Quebec City on December 18, 1927. The occasion was the "coming-out" of the debutante niece of the Lieutenant-Governor, Narcisse Peredeau. Governor-General Viscount Willingdon and Lady Willingdon were present as guests of honour.

The council chambers were transformed into a replica of the rooms of the Versailles Palace. Hanging from the great arched windows were baskets of ferns and flowers. Below these were marble busts of prominent people resting on pedestals. Against this opulent background were one thousand people, all in costume. Special trains had brought them from Montreal, Toronto and other places across Canada. Upon entering, the guests

The Pfeiffer family business, Quebec City

passed in a long line in front of the dais as an equerry announced the name of the character each person represented. Most were historic royalty or aristocrats of France or England. There were amusing juxtapositions of characters, as when the revolutionary François Villon danced with Marie Antoinette. A great deal of research was required to ensure that the costumes and accessories were accurate. No two were alike, because each guest had to register their choice ahead of time, and duplicates were forbidden. Nineteen-year-old Harold went as Simon Fraser, Lord Lovat, and enjoyed himself immensely, indulging his love of costume, dancing and parties all at the same time.

A disastrous fire at the family business, followed immediately by the crash of 1929, catapulted the Pfeiffer family from affluence to genteel poverty. The considerable real estate property which Adolphus had acquired plunged in value along with everyone else's. He was forced to sell most of his property at rock-bottom prices in order to meet his obligations and attempt to salvage something from the disaster. In the end, Pfeiffer managed to rebuild his plant with the help of friends. He had not been physically hurt by the fire, but it was a devastating blow to the spirit, and he never recovered his *joie de vivre*. The business survived but did not thrive, and he died at sixty-five in 1935.

At the time of the disaster, Harold had just begun working at Price Brothers' pulp and paper mill. As the last one hired, he was immediately let go due to retrenchment because of the depression.

Dr. Marius Barbeau, folklorist, ethnologist, 1958

Sculpting, Antiques and Marius Barbeau

From 1925 to 1927, Harold attended night classes in modelling at the Ecole des Beaux Arts in Quebec City, first under Professor Jan Bailleul, the Belgian sculptor, and then Sylvia D'Aoust. Bailleul gave him a good deal of encouragement, but he left the school, and D'Aoust took over. Harold thenceforward received little support and no constructive attention. He feels this was because he was an anglophone in a francophone institution.

"There was considerable animosity at the art school; I was the only English speaking student in my class, and my work rarely received favourable criticism from my teachers. French speaking students seemed always to get the honours regardless of their merit."

During his time at the Beaux Arts, he met Marius Barbeau, the legendary anthropologist, musicologist and folklorist of the National Museum, who offered Harold support and encouragement and persuaded him to research arts and crafts in remote parts of Quebec.

While he still lived in Quebec City, Harold frequently visited Ottawa. Sometimes he would stay with the Barbeau family, which he particularly enjoyed because he had access to Dr. Barbeau's personal collection of masks, rattles, drums and other artifacts. He could actually handle them and hear Barbeau tell the stories of their origin and use.

Dr. C. Marius Barbeau

It was a special pleasure when Barbeau took up a drum and beat it and sang an Indian chant. When he spoke from his knowledge of many cultures and dialects as he showed his precious artifacts, they returned to life in Harold's imagination.

"Everywhere I looked, on the grand piano, the tables, the mantlepiece, the walls and on the living room floor, there were fascinating objects which he had accumulated in his many trips studying Indian culture across Canada and in the United States. There were early carvings by François Jobin and more recent work by André Bourgault of St. Jean Port Joli in Quebec. There were beautiful argillite carvings by the great Charles Edenshaw, the Haida Indian carver of Skidegate on Queen Charlotte Island. There were some huge glass globes which had washed up on the B.C. coast, having broken away from Japanese fish nets and floated across the Pacific. A most beautiful Chilkat blanket had a place of honour on one wall, and there were intricately carved Kwakiutl rattles on a table." This dense clutter of art and artifacts appears to have made a lasting impression. Harold's home today is crowded from top to bottom with paintings, photographs, native artifacts and of course, his own works.

In a large bay window seat was a splendid collection of decorated pottery bowls, glazed in blues and black on the turkey-red terracotta base, made by Emily Carr. Barbeau had purchased them many years ago when he first met the artist at her home. He was one of the first to recognise and foster her great talent as a painter, potter, hooked rug maker, designer and writer.

"His collection of paintings by his friends, Lismer, Jackson, Harris, Pepper, Langdon Kihn, Emily Carr, Jean Paul Lemieux, and my brother Gordon Pfeiffer was of great interest to me, for I knew most of them.

"Dr. Barbeau was both a gentle man and a fine gentleman. He was soft spoken and did not care for arguments. He never swore and perhaps felt more comfortable with ladies than men. He was temperate but enjoyed a little good wine."

Saturday was almost a holy day for Dr. Barbeau. He would lie in bed all afternoon listening to the Metropolitan Opera. There were to be no phone calls, no interruptions

12

of any kind, and any visiting grandchildren knew of this private time and respected it. His great love of music had been nurtured by his mother, who was an accomplished pianist, and his ear for music stood him in good stead when he started collecting folk songs, especially because he could also write music. His vast collection of folksongs, mainly of French Canada, recorded on wax cylinders, is of world importance. It is stored at the Canadian Museum of Civilization in Hull, Quebec.

In the '30s, Harold went on several collecting trips with him, looking for good examples of weaving and carving and early French-Canadian furniture. About this time, the art of finger-weaving in Canada was almost extinct. For generations, the *habitant* women used to weave *jarretières* (garters) to hold up their husbands' stockings. A few of the more enterprising women wove beautiful *ceintures flechées* (arrow sashes). These were greatly prized, woven mostly in reds, yellow and blue, in a pattern of chevrons, like stylized arrowheads, about ten inches wide, with long fringes, in all about twelve feet long. They were worn by the merchants and other prominent men in the towns. The more affluent men wore fur coats, usually made of racoon or muskrat hides, known as *capots de chats,* and on special occasions the gentry would sport their handsome sashes. Since it appeared that this type of weaving was dying out, Dr. Barbeau and a few other concerned people persuaded the nuns in a Montreal convent to learn the art and teach it to their students.

"In 1935 or '36, Dr. Barbeau wrote a monograph on arrow sashes. He knew of my interest in weaving and encouraged me to go to Les Eboulements and St. Hilarion down the St. Lawrence and have several of the ladies who still did this weaving teach it to me. I took his advice and was later able to describe to him the details of sash weaving; the length of strands required, the shrinkage which resulted as one progresses with the finger weaving and the arrangement of colours to produce a given design."

The monograph was published by the museum, entitled *Assomption Sash* (Bulletin 93, Anthropological Series 24). There are many illustrations in the monograph, some of which are garters and ties which Harold made. It is still available from the Museum of Civilization.

Dr. Barbeau arranged concerts at which country folk sang and danced to the accompaniment of violins and accordions played in the traditional style by the older men. There was a revival of interest in the folklore of Quebec, and Barbeau encouraged many younger men and women singers to perform at public concerts, and many went on to professional careers.

Barbeau took copious notes as he studied the Indians in the United States and more particularly Indian tribes in British Columbia, especially their mythology, customs, dialects, music and songs. His notes were a mixture of his own brand of shorthand, English, French and Latin, sprinkled with Indian words and phrases. Consequently, his scratchings were almost indecipherable, and only a trained specialist could transcribe or interpret them. He sometimes used a bird quill which he himself fashioned into a pen. So fine was his writing that a couple of pages of his notes, transcribed into French or English, would comprise a full size chapter.

One summer, Sir Ernest MacMillan, the composer and conductor of the Toronto Symphony Orchestra, accompanied Dr. Barbeau out to the British Columbia coast, where they recorded many native songs, chants and music. Sir Ernest taught him how to record the non-European form of music on paper. Up to this time, few people had made recordings, and it must have been a remarkable sight to see Dr. Barbeau carrying his cumbersome Edison phonograph with its horn, recording the voices of the natives on wax cylinders.

In the 1930s, Dr. Barbeau was very friendly with the Director of the Detroit Museum, where he had given illustrated talks on French Canada and its arts and crafts. Under his guidance, the director made several exploratory trips down the St. Lawrence with Dr. Barbeau, purchasing fine examples of 17th and 18th century furniture, made by French Canadian artisans, for the Detroit Museum. They also collected church and secular silver made by early French settlers and by United Empire Loyalists who had migrated to eastern Canada from New England.

Dr. Barbeau made many fruitless efforts to persuade the museum and government authorities to start acquiring these rare and precious objects. American and some Canadian private collectors were quicker to realize their value. It was only in the late 1950s that Prime Minister Diefenbaker became interested, and decided that a Historical Division should be established at the Museum of Man and that they should start collecting good examples of early Canadiana for posterity.

In 1932-33, when Barbeau was researching the painter Cornelius Krieghoff, Harold located more than eighty previously unknown works by the artist in Montreal and Quebec City. He photographed and catalogued them, and recorded them in the *catalogue raisonée* in Barbeau's first book on Krieghoff, *Cornelius Krieghoff, Pioneer Painter of North America*, published in 1934 by MacMillan.

During the same period, Harold also acted as an agent for William Watson, the first man to open a commercial art gallery in Montreal and probably the greatest authority on Krieghoff at the time, purchasing many paintings for museums and private collections.

When Krieghoff lived in Quebec, he taught art at Miss Brown's School for Young Ladies. It was not uncommon for amateur painters to copy the master's oils, and on occasion, the name Cornelius Krieghoff appeared on the canvas. He is known to have painted many potboilers and it became an art in itself to identify originals. Many paintings were sent to Dr. Barbeau for scrutiny, and Harold was also frequently consulted for his opinion.

"I have a pastel drawing, *Council Rock, Lake Lagon, Quebec*, which was done in 1854 by Charlotte Victoria Houghton when she was a pupil at Miss Brown's. Parts of the picture are remarkably similar to Krieghoff's manner of painting and I suspect that he did a little touching-up while making his rounds of the students.

"When I was on staff at the Museum of Man in Ottawa, I was mounting a display of some Victorian rooms, using the artifacts and furnishings of the period. I used illustrations of Krieghoff paintings to check for authenticity. Many of his paintings were actual portraits of the owners and of their horses and sleighs. They were so delicately done and representational that they provided an accurate reference.

"While I was working at the museum, important anthropologists or scientists often visited, and Dr. Barbeau sometimes asked them to his home for the evening. He would frequently say to me, 'You will come along also. If I suggested I might be imposing, he would say, `You are part of the family. I shall expect you.'

"I was with him when Allan Jarvis, the Director of the National Gallery at the time, phoned to tell him that he had been selected for the Order of Canada. He was almost shocked and said, 'Are you sure? This is a most beautiful honour.' He immediately phoned his wife and daughters with the exciting news."

Harold's friendship with Dr. Barbeau and his family was very close, and he learned a great deal from him. The respect for the down-to-earth qualities of Habitants and native peoples, and the appreciation of the importance of recording and preserving what could be salvaged of their cultures as they changed irrevocably, the meticulous approach to collecting and research: all are gifts of the empathy between Barbeau and Pfeiffer.

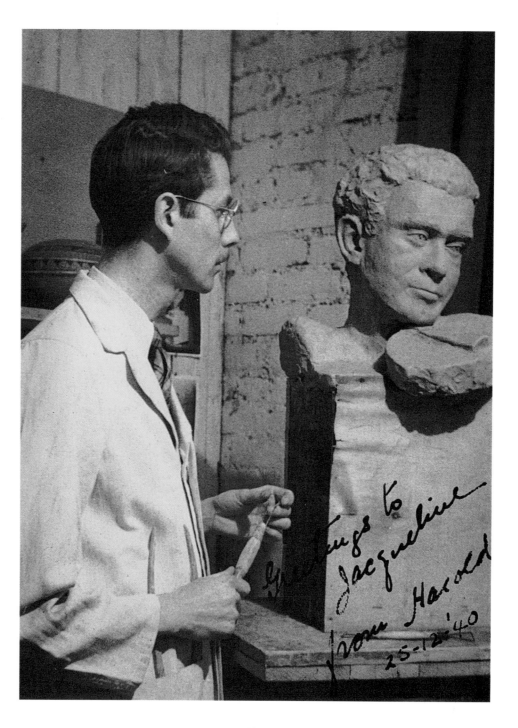

Harold with his portrait of violinist Arthur Leblanc, 1939

Work: Jobs, Commissions and a Career

The depression was on in earnest, and work was not to be had. After helping out awhile with the reconstructed family business, doing odd jobs, Harold decided to invest his savings in a year abroad, learning what he could from the artistic treasures of Europe and the considerably more sophisticated artistic communities to be found there. He spent six months in London, in 1930, studying antique and modern sculptures in the British Museum, the Victoria and Albert, and the Tate Gallery. Living a year in Paris, in 1931, visiting and studying the treasures of the Louvre and the work of living artists in the galleries and workshops, Harold was exposed to the original sculptures of Eric Gill, Jacob Epstein and Auguste Rodin, among others, confirming his preference for realism as the style that most suited him.

Harold attended daily classes at the Louvre in interior design and decoration, and spent his evenings and weekends enjoying the wealth of cultural experiences available even to impecunious students.

"In Paris I got to know some young art students and they persuaded me to move over to the *"Boul Mich,"* the *Boulevard St. Michel*, where the pensions were cheaper and some of the restaurants catered to students with low incomes and big appetites.

Harold's crafts: batiks, terracotta figures, finger-woven ties, lamp and candle sconce

I particularly remember a Russian restaurant called the K'NAM, which served a wonderful huge bowl of borscht for only a few francs.

"There were always art exhibitions nearby to go to, and we never missed the free ones. We would discuss the merits of each artist well into the night, sometimes feeling that one of our group did far superior work, even if their teachers did not feel they were so interesting.

"At least once a week a party was arranged to which all contributed: fresh bread, cheese and wine. These were noisy, chatty affairs. The French love talking.

"At the *Beaux Arts* in Quebec City, the teachers emphasised the importance of doing realistic detailed work on the model, creating a vivid impression of character and showing a close biological resemblance to the subject: 'It must look like him, not his brother!' Most of the work in the exhibitions we saw in Paris was much broader, often rather like cartoons or caricatures. Yes, we argued!"

Returning to Canada in 1931 from his year abroad, Harold did some unpaid experimental work with native clays for the Director-General of *Arts Domestique* of the Quebec Ministry of Agriculture, hoping it would lead to a paying job. He tested and recorded the response of various clays to firing and glazing, in order to identify those that would be suitable for pottery and modelling.

"I became friendly with a potter from Brittany who was teaching in Quebec. He encouraged me to do some work on a kick-wheel which he loaned me. I made several pots and figurines and had them fired. Several of my pieces exploded, the heat being too much for some of the clays I was testing. One subject was from the popular book *Maria Chapdelaine*, and I did a figurine of Maria picking potatoes and another of the lazy farmer Edwige Legare resting by the roadside. I have both still in my collection."

Lack of a paying job forced him to exploit his crafts skills to produce anything that would sell, from batik scarves and fingerwoven ties to lamps, terracotta masks and figures and greeting cards, anything that brought in a few dollars. He became a creative scavenger, using clinkers from the furnace, which resembled ancient rock formations, as bases for artificial bonsai trees. He cut out sheets of brass and pewter in the form of fir trees laden with snow for candle sconces.

He travelled periodically to Montreal, trying to interest some of the more exclusive shops in his batiks. He always took the opportunity to visit antiquarian book shops to look through their prints, etchings and engravings. "Usually I could find one or two which I felt would interest people in Quebec City. My friends the Darcy sisters always seemed to be able to dispose of them in their little shop at a profit for both parties. I never discovered a Rembrandt, but once, in New York, I found a batch of early Quebec Bartlett prints and two Currier and Ives prints, which were a bonanza for me."

Harold financed trips to New York by rooting around in the junk shops there and bringing back overlooked treasures to sell in Quebec City. He had a real eye for women's fashions, and made it a point to visit Bloomingdale's basement, where very high quality goods which were slightly past the peak of fashion in New York, and therefore coming into fashion in places like Quebec, were to be had for next to nothing. "I would buy two or three dresses at $6.95 each, and the Darcy sisters would sell them for twenty or more. I never had any capital to finance any more than a few dresses at a time, but I managed to make enough to go on with. I was taking care of myself and not being a burden on my family."

In the summer season, he got permission to set himself up in the lobby of the Manoir Richelieu in Murray Bay to do some sculpting. He hoped to get some portrait commissions but only managed to get a surly young boy. When the boy was not posing, Harold modelled masks of Indians which were sold in the gift shop nearby. When the Manoir officially closed for the season, he moved his work to Chamard's Lorne House, a comfortable old log hotel where the Pfeiffers had always stayed during visits to Murray Bay in their years of prosperity.

"At the end of the season, I was the only guest there when a young lawyer came for the weekend. All his Montreal friends had left the resort, and there was only me to talk to. We discovered that we had attended some of the same parties in Montreal, though we had never met. At the time I was travelling to Montreal quite frequently to attend dances and some "coming-out" balls. We had some pleasant chats and a number of long walks and went swimming in the Manoir pool. The young man was Pierre Elliot Trudeau, who later became prime minister of Canada."

Charlevoix County and its back ranges was very familiar to Harold. He had spent many weekends on sketching tours with his brother Gordon, often accompanied by other artist friends, including George Pepper, Kay Daly, Jean Palardy, Jori Smith, René Richard or Bob Pilot. He frequently spent holidays and weekends in Cap à l'aigle, Les Eboulements, St. Simeon and Tadoussac, and the country became very familiar and dearly loved.

"Our rendezvous was frequently at St. Hilarion, where our close friend Jean Palardy lived. He was a raconteur, painter, historical researcher, bon vivant and a very jolly fellow to be with. He did considerable work on the vast restoration of Fort Louisbourg on Cape Breton Island, and was the author of a massive volume on the early furniture of French Canada. On most weekends when we went down there, Jean would arrange a square dance. He would be the M.C. and caller. These were always memorable occasions."

Years later, at the outbreak of World War II, the National Film Board produced a propaganda film in French, shot on location in St. Jean, on Isle d'Orleans. This was familiar territory for Harold, who had spent many weekends with his brothers in the cottage of André Bieler, the painter. At Marius Barbeau's suggestion, Harold was engaged as liaison and interpreter, smoothing the film crew's way with the local habitants.

For a time, Harold augmented his income by trading in antiques. "Every Saturday morning I made the rounds of junk shops, picking up odds and ends. Some required a bit of polish or a touch of paint. A beautiful old framed mirror lacked the odd rosette or garland, so I made moulds of the good parts, cast new ones, glued them on and gilded them: hey presto, a magnificent antique for an elegant home!"

Harold went to work as an interior decorator with Simpson's Avon House in Toronto, and began executing sculptural portraits of prominent Canadians. He attended Central Technical School in Toronto, where he studied pottery with Mrs. Peter Haworth. He also began moving in the society of other artists, soaking up support and influence wherever he found it.

He met the sculptors Frances Loring and Florence Wyle, who encouraged him to keep on with his sculpting at a time when he was discouraged and considering giving it up. He pursued further studies in design and handicrafts and in the making of theatrical and decorative masks, at the New York School of Decorating.

Dolph Pfeiffer died in 1935, and Harold moved home to be with his mother. He picked up some decorating work, and completed three portrait busts, including one of Captain Joseph Bernier, who had taken the icebreaker *Arctic* into uncharted northern waters, and claimed them for Canada. Unfortunately the captain died just before the portrait was finished.

"I did a heroic bust of Capt. Bernier wearing a bearskin coat with his head partially covered by the hood. There was a delay in finishing it in Levis because of his illness and death. Madame Bernier loaned me many photographs and I finished it at our country home at Lac Beauport. Wanting the approval of his widow and his brother, I asked them to come out to see it. Madame Bernier wept when she saw it, and said *"C'est lui, c'est vraiment lui, c'est lui en vie!"* (It's him, it's really him, it's him in life!) and M. Bernier was equally pleased with its monumental character.

"I cast it in plaster and Dr. Paul Rainville, Director of the Quebec Museum, came to see it and was very taken with it, and said that it was a great figure of a national hero and that it should certainly be acquired for the museum collection. I duly sent them photographs and asked the acquisition committee to come and see it. They would not purchase it. Mr. Rainville was very upset about this and was told that the St. Jean Baptiste Society had decided against it because it had not been done by *un de chez nous*. Mr. Rainville was quite shocked and his description of some of the committee members was quite unprintable. He did say, however, 'we'll eventually get it.'

"I stored it in the basement of my brother's house in Sillery. Then, over a long weekend, when no-one was at home, a sudden rainstorm and flash flood left more than a foot of water in the basement. The plaster cast was completely soaked and had absorbed a lot of water. After it was thoroughly dried out, the surface, with much of the detail, cracked and crumbled off. All I have is a rather fuzzy photo of it."

A couple of jobs in sales, at Simpson's department store and in Eatons' art gallery, convinced Harold and his employers that he was not cut out to be a salesman. "I wasn't aggressive enough. If a customer wanted to buy something, I was happy to discuss it, and help make a choice, but I was no good at persuasion, at getting them to buy something when they weren't sure they wanted it."

Moving on to more appropriate employment, Harold went to work in 1938 at the Baraud Studio, a distinguished interior design firm in Toronto, where he learned to do oriental lacquer work, and got the chance to exercise his artistic skills and judgement.

Two sculptors in Toronto whose work Harold admired

Yousuf Karsh, celebrated photographer, 1949

were Frances Loring and Florence Wyle. They had acquired an abandoned church and converted it into a studio-home. It became the rendezvous for many of Toronto's artists, architects, musicians, writers, scientists and many up-and-coming young people of artistic bent. They were an eccentric couple for the Toronto of that time, independent and big-hearted. They were referred to as the Loring-Wyles or more familiarly as "The Girls."

Harold was first taken to the Loring-Wyles by his musician friends Murray and Frances Adaskin, when he was working in Toronto in 1934. It was generally understood that, when invited to one of their parties, one asked, "and what can I bring along?" Food was always welcome. Like most artists, they had many ups and downs; sculpture commissions were not always to be had. Harold went to the parties they often held after openings at the Royal Canadian Academy and Ontario Society of Artists exhibitions. "They had their troubles, but they survived hard times and became two of the finest sculptors in Canada. They were two most remarkable women."

Their work is exhibited in the National Gallery and the Art Gallery of Ontario. Florence Wyle did the Edith Cavell memorial in Toronto, and Frances Loring did the

Banting and Best portraits. Another major work is Frances Loring's bronze statue of Sir Robert Borden which stands outside the Houses of Parliament on Capital Hill in Ottawa. She beat Harold for the commission in 1943.

"Some years later, when I was working in Toronto, I went over quite often just for tea and a chat. I frequently brought over photographs of my work and asked for their criticism, which I knew would be candid but of real value, and which I greatly appreciated. When I moved temporarily out to Edmonton, they kindly let me store my plaster heads and busts at their studio. Among the interesting people I met there was the outstanding violinist Adolph Koldofsky, a lovely fellow!"

Another influence in Harold's development as a sculptor was Leo Mol, master ceramist, painter and stained-glass designer and perhaps Canada's most important sculptor. Mol received commissions to design and execute many memorials and statues, among them the last three Popes.

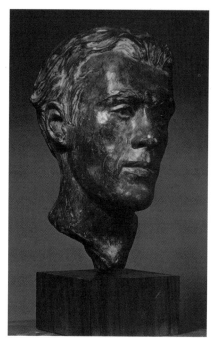

Ross Pratt, pianist, Montreal 1939

The City of Winnipeg has created the Leo Mol Sculpture Garden to honour him. Some sixty-five of his smaller sculptures, along with many of his paintings and ceramic figurines and stained-glass designs, are housed in a specially designed pavilion. Twenty-five of his larger bronzes are displayed in the garden alongside a reflecting pool.

"It is wonderful that the city has chosen to honour Mol, especially as he is able to appreciate the thanks while he is still with us. We have been close friends for almost forty years and I am always his guest when I am in Winnipeg, as he is mine when he stays in Ottawa. Over the years his advice and criticism have been of great value to me. He is a great artist. In 1989 he received the Order of Canada."

The Pfeiffers were a very musical family, and over the years Harold has met many instrumentalists and singers, whose memories he treasures. He was eager to sculpt some internationally-known artists. In 1939 he sculpted busts of two close friends, Ross Pratt, the pianist and Arthur LeBlanc, the violinist. The Pratt bust stands up today as one of Harold's most successful portraits. As his career developed, his ambition was realised as he came into contact with international figures in the world of music, and completed busts of contralto Portia White, violist William Primrose and pianist Vladimir Ashkenazy.

Sculptors Florence Wyle(l) and Frances Loring(r) in their Toronto studio

Mrs. Peggy McKay with Harold and *War Worker*, 1941

War Work and More

When World War II came, Harold was rejected for war service because of his health; he was forty pounds underweight, wore glasses and had a heart murmur. He went to stay in Les Eboulements, at a country hotel famous for its wonderful food, with the express intention of gaining weight. He ate enormous amounts of very rich foods, including ice cream for breakfast, and after three weeks had gained one quarter of a pound.

In one of the first engagements of the war with the Japanese, Hong Kong was taken. Most of Harold's contemporaries from Quebec were in reserve units of the Royal Rifles Regiment, and had been hastily mobilized and sent to Hong Kong with no combat experience and very little training. The death toll was appalling and those who survived were taken prisoner, eventually to return malnourished, many crippled, most to suffer ill health for the rest of their lives. It was embarrassing and unpleasant, to say the least, to be walking the streets of the combatants' home town, a young anglophone man with a German name, in apparently good health, and not in uniform.

He eventually signed on with the Inspection Board of the U.K. and Canada, and went to work at a munitions plant, inspecting bombs, primers and fuses, in Valcartier,

Harold in the Studio
Building, Toronto 1940

Quebec. In 1941 he transferred from Montreal to Toronto, assigned to work in the X-ray
department at General Engineering in Scarborough. He lived in Lawren Harris' Studio
Building on Severn Street, renting the studio of Kay Daly and George Pepper.

"As our work was very dangerous, handling amatol and tetrol and other extremely
volatile explosives, everyone had to wear linen jump-suits with buttons down the sides to
minimize the risk of friction and sparks. We wore special shoes, no jewellery was permitted, and even our spectacles had to be kept captive. A spark could end it for all of us."

The plant employed some 16,000 people. Noticing the bare walls of the dining hall
and lounge, Harold got permission to mount monthly art shows. He borrowed works
from artist friends, and mounted one-person exhibitions by Roloff Beny, Kay Daly,
George Pepper and Nicholas Hornyansky.

Harold first met Roloff Beny at the University of Toronto, where Beny was an architecture student. "There was an exhibition of his paintings at Hart House, mostly western
scenes of grain elevators, abandoned old houses, ghost towns and the lonely prairie
itself. His work was very realistic. He had not yet evolved the more mystical poetic
renderings he did later."

One day, sitting in the cafeteria at the plant having lunch, he found himself alongside
a lady with a strong Scottish accent, Mrs. Peggy McKay of Glasgow. Another lady,
sitting across from them, said she had just received news that her husband had been
killed. Her only son had been killed in Italy some months earlier. Harold found this

woman's tale distressing enough, and then Mrs. McKay told her story. She said her husband was blown up in a naval bombardment, her sister killed in the London blitz, and her eighteen-year-old son was missing at sea. Three uncles and ten cousins were lost on a trawler torpedoed at sea three weeks after war broke out. Among the 16,000 employees there were many terribly sad stories, but this was almost inconceivably tragic.

"I was very moved by her story, which I just could not get out of my mind. I wondered how I could perhaps let her story be known; how she was stoutly contributing so much to the war effort while so many grudgingly offered so little. I decided to sculpt a life-size bust of her, posing just as she was, examining fuses.

"Mrs. McKay agreed to pose for me over a few weekends in her small low-rent row house. The modelling progressed and she enjoyed it as much as I did. It was a therapy which she really needed. Here was a woman of exceptional courage; with all her memories of her departed loved ones, she carried on her work in a very cheerful manner. The bust was called *War Worker* and upon its completion, it received much favourable comment.

Lieutenant Harold Pfeiffer in uniform at last, 1944

27

"In creating a piece of sculpture it is considered good composition to design it so that its lines or profiles are attractive from any point of view. To do this successfully, it is often necessary to model a form anatomically correctly, as in the nude, and then dress the model. It sounds peculiar, but in so doing, you get the impression of a human body under the costume.

"I tried to make this piece as simple and classical as possible. All unnecessary folds and creases have been eliminated. The bust features a woman in industry. At first glance the eye is focused on the line from the eyes, down the fold in her uniform to the fuse in her hand. The eye then goes along and up her arm, circling around down the other arm to the fuse again. All negative lines or dark shadows,

Portia White sitting
for Harold, 1944

which tend to make a work fussy or agitate the eyes, have been eliminated,
but I've placed a few folds in definite places so as to create a circular motion,
encompassing the piece as a whole."

Harold began to suffer from severe respiratory illness, caused by the rampant ragweed
growing all around the plant and the fumes of amatol and tetrol inside, and the medical
staff were eventually persuaded to seek a replacement. He finally joined the special services
as a craft specialist, to supervise and teach in Hobby Lobbies for the Army and Air Force,
under the auspices of YMCA War Services. An exhibition of arts and crafts that he helped
organize at the plant had attracted the attention of the military authorities, who were casting
about for people to organize creative recreational activities for military personnel. He was
eventually to wear the uniforms of a captain in the army and a flight lieutenant in the air force.

In 1944 Harold was on his way by train to Halifax where he was arranging an exhibition of handicrafts by his pupils in the Air Force at #31, Personnel Depot in Moncton,
New Brunswick. Sitting across the aisle from him was a lady immersed in a musical score.
He had read concert reviews about a black contralto who was receiving raves for her
magnificent singing. Watching her, and waiting for an opportune time to talk to her, he
noticed the gold initials "P.W." on the handbag at her feet. He decided this must indeed
be Portia White. When his interest is piqued, Harold Pfeiffer is not shy. He introduced
himself and they had an agreeable chat for almost two hours. She showed considerable
interest in his work.

One of Harold's jobs as an officer at the Air Force base was arranging entertainment. Saturday night was always dance night. He describes the music as mostly noise, with a little rhythm, employing guitars, saxophones, traps and sometimes a fiddle. Because the available musicians were all transients, the composition of the band was always changing. In any case, the lads seemed more interested in the busloads of young and not-so-young ladies Harold rounded up as dancing partners for them. However, among the dozens of young men were some whom Harold felt might appreciate a classical concert by a fine artist.

"I asked Miss White if she would honour us, if I could arrange an evening of classical music and song. She thought that her agent and the union would agree to her participation in such a concert 'for free and for the troops.' She was to be visiting in Moncton for ten days the following month. I was delighted with her generous support and asked her if she would pose for me for her portrait while she was in Moncton. She said she would be honoured. What luck!

"I arranged some good publicity and we were given permission to invite the citizens of the town to the concert. One of my fellow officers was a fine pianist, and had accompanied several prominent concert artists in London before joining the Air Force, and he agreed to accompany her. We had a full house, and after the concert, a splendid reception was given Miss White at the officers' mess."

While she was sitting for Harold, she told him about a sculptor she knew in New York whom she felt he must meet. He was Richmond Barthé, destined to become the best-known black sculptor in America. Many internationally-known figures had posed for him and his work was to be found in many art museums in America and in important private collections.

"Miss White wrote to him that I would be spending about ten days at Christmas-time in New York and, to my astonishment, he wrote asking me to be his guest at his studio-home. I was a bit shy about accepting this 'sight-unseen' invitation, but Miss White had a keen sense of personalities, and when she wrote to him, she had sent along a photograph of the bust I had sculpted of her. I visited with him for a week, and it was a most memorable time for me. This chance encounter with Barthé changed the course of my career. For many years in our correspondence he continually encouraged me to continue sculpting."

At the time, Harold was discouraged by the reception his sculptures were receiving. It was Barthé who talked him out of his funk and told him, "You have a rare gift from God and you must continue sculpting." At the time of Harold's visit, Barthé was working on the male nude shown in the photograph, and he insisted that a thorough knowledge of anatomy was essential to successful portraiture. He also pointed out that Harold's gifts included his gregarious nature, which would open doors and create opportunities all his life. Harold began to realize that his propensity for "people-collecting" was a valuable talent.

Barthé's studio was a fourth floor walk-up in a warehouse. He had converted one end into a comfortable apartment. The ceiling was high, permitting him to sculpt figures of

Richmond Barthé

Male nude by Barthé

Female nude by Barthé

heroic dimensions. When Harold was there, he had just completed sculpting the bust of Dr. Booker T. Washington and had several nude figures in various stages of completion.

Besides being an accomplished sculptor, Barthé was a pianist and a painter as well. He was also intensely interested in the ballet and theatre. Many well-known actors spent free time at his studio, including Vincent Price, John Gielgud, Helen Hayes and Lawrence Olivier.

Several years later, Barthé moved to Jamaica and invited Harold to visit him. He had a house at St. Annes, Fern Valley, near Ocho Rios, and a hideaway studio up on the hill behind his home. He had temporarily abandoned sculpting and was concentrating on painting.

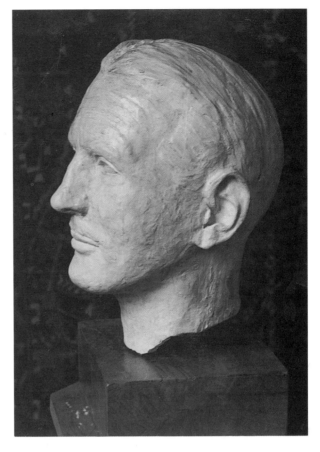

William Primrose, violist, 1947

'Shortly after this, Barthé received several interesting commissions in California and decided to move out there. We corresponded for some time before he passed away. I will always be grateful for the support and advice he gave me. He was a true friend and a remarkably fine artist.'

Another artist who gravitated to Barthé's studio was the great Swedish sculptor Carl Milles, who was teaching at Cranbrooke Academy in Bloomfield Hills, Michigan at the time. It was he who introduced fountains to many American cities; his use of water in large pools, graced with bronze nude youths, delighted millions of people. After visiting in New York, Harold was on his way to Windsor and Detroit to see friends. Barthé insisted that he meet Carl Milles at Cranbrooke. Harold arrived as Milles was showing Cleve Horne, a sculptor from Toronto, around the place. After Horne left, Pfeiffer was invited to stay for lunch.

"This was the first time I made the acquaintance of the work of Georgia O'Keefe. On the walls were four huge paintings of enlarged flowers, bright orangey-red hibiscus, the palest sensuous petals of lillies resembling ballet dancers in long white gowns. After luncheon, Mr. Milles brought me across to his large studio. Students and helpers were

31

building armatures or doing rough modelling on a series of nude resurrection sculptures for a cemetery. This was a most memorable experience, a visit of the greatest importance to me.

"After taking me on a tour of the grounds to view some of his more important sculptures, set in alcoves of high cedars to highlight the white marble or bronze, and the long pool of water where many sensuous bronze nymphs cavorted in front of the library, we returned to his house for tea. I was mentally exhausted and in seventh heaven!

"Before leaving, Mr. Milles gave me an illustrated brochure of his studio-home near Stockholm which is called Millesgarden. I had never been to Scandinavia, but the following year, I went to visit friends there and made sure I included Stockholm and Millesgarden. Much to my disappointment, Mr. Milles had not returned from Rome, where he spent the winter months. He was nearing eighty and his health and eyesight were deteriorating. I never saw him again and he passed away shortly after this. I was very grateful to Barthé for introducing me to a great artist and a charming gentleman."

"On one occasion, in France, I spent four wonderful days in Saché, near Tours, at the studio of the late Jo Davidson, whose work I had so admired as a boy. The manor was owned by his son, Jean. Jean's brother was married to the daughter of the famous American sculptor Calder, known for his mobiles. They lived on the hill above the manor. Jean and his wife were most hospitable, and when they heard that his father had been an idol of mine, the studio keys were just handed to me. Here I saw the bulk of the original plaster casts of the many important people in Europe and America who had sat for him from 1912 to 1930. Recently, in Washington, at the National Gallery, I was delighted to see a special room devoted to some twenty of Davidson's bronze portrait busts. They also had several busts by my friend Barthé."

When the war ended, Harold joined the staff of Macdonald College of McGill University in 1945, and taught Arts & Crafts and Interior Decoration until 1949. He also taught crafts at summer camps in 1948, '49 and '50. William Primrose, the Scottish violist, was one of the most prominent of his day, and for a few weeks in 1947 he gave Master Classes at Macdonald College. Harold asked him to sit for a portrait. Primrose did not have a remarkable appearance, but his prominence as a musician made him an attractive subject.

> "He agreed to pose for his bust and we had three sittings. He said that he would pose for longer periods but his protective wife objected and said that he must rest. I needed three more sittings to complete it. He was to play at the Tanglewood Festival in Pittsfield, Massachusetts and agreed to pose for me down there. It was difficult for him to free his time between rehearsals and the performance. The end result was that we only had one sitting and I was not satisfied. His time was precious, as he was to leave almost immediately for Scotland to play at the Edinburgh Festival the following week. He agreed to give me a sitting or two at the Julliard School of Music in New York, where he was a faculty member. When it was finally finished, I exhibited the bust at the Montreal Museum of Fine Arts that autumn."

In 1951 and 1952, Pfeiffer taught English to francophone cadets at the Royal Military College in St. Jean sur Richelieu. His students were not serious about learning English, and it was a frustrating job. However, he made friends among the officer-instructors, and enjoyed some excellent skiing holidays in nearby Vermont. When he heard of an opening at Morgan's department store for an interior decorator, Harold jumped at it.

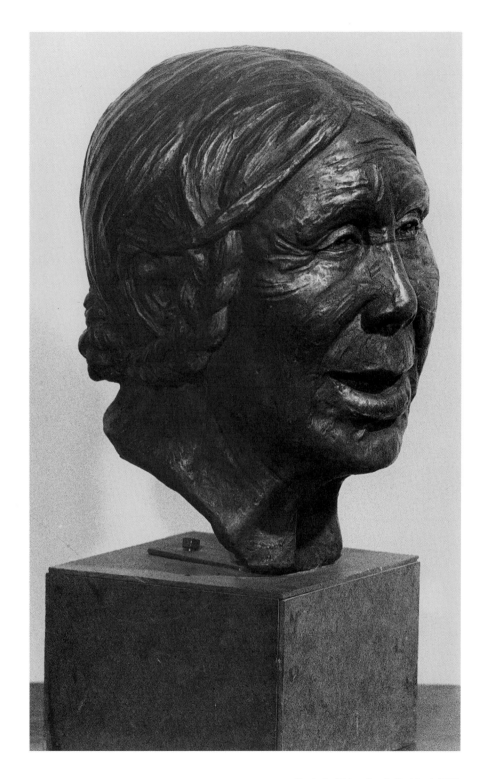

Ooah, Frobisher Bay, Baffin Island, 1956

First Encounters with Arctic People

During the early 1950s, Harold's friend Jim Houston, the artist, who with his wife Alma was a pioneer in developing Inuit art co-operatives, suggested he join the Department of Northern Affairs to work with tuberculosis patients in hospitals and rehabilitation centres in the arctic. Houston was working with the department in Baffin Island as an administrator in Cape Dorset.

At the time, Harold was enjoying work as a decorator in Montreal. The government advertised for someone with his qualifications and Jim encouraged him to try for the position. It was tantalizing, but Harold declined because the salary offered was less than he was making at decorating work. No one was appointed that year. Houston kept after him, and the next year the same position was advertised again, with a better salary. Harold still did not feel it was sufficient, given the isolation he would have to endure, and the amenities he would have to do without.

"The day before the competition closed, I received a call from the department asking why I had not applied. I told them the salary was still far too low. They had interviewed other applicants but none were suitable. They said they would augment my salary if I would agree to teach English to natives for six hours a week in addition to full time rehabilitation work. I agreed, on the stipulation that I not sit at a desk all year. I wanted to travel and live with the people for some time each year. They agreed, and I held them to it."

In 1954 Harold was engaged to provide a form of occupational therapy for both Indians and Inuit at the Hôpital du Parc Savard in Quebec City. His oldest brother, Dr. Walter Pfeiffer, was a lung specialist working there. A self-effacing, compassionate and tireless worker, Walter compiled a dictionary of Inuit phrases concerning health problems, illustrated with his own drawings. Harold's job was to teach and encourage the patients to do handicrafts, to help them forget their illness and their loneliness. Their separation from all that was familiar was very painful for them.

The patients that Harold worked with were Inuit from Northern Quebec, Labrador, the Hudson's Bay area and Baffin Island. Tuberculosis was rife among them, as they had as yet developed no immunity to European diseases. There were no treatment facilities in the north, so they had to be brought south to recover. The flight south was only the first of a series of shocks for them. At that time the majority were living in igloos and tents, heated and lit by a kudlik, a soapstone stove, fuelled with seal oil, with a wick of wild cotton or moss.

Illya of Cape Dorset, Baffin Island, 1954

36

They had never been away from their birthplace settlements, except into the arctic wilderness, and entering a hospital with white-clad doctors and nurses, being put into bed with cotton sheets, electric light at the flick of a switch, and having strange meals brought to them was a very new and frightening experience. Most of them covered their heads with their pillows and cried for several days. Harold's job was to lift their spirits by giving them something creative to do.

Aside from the therapeutic benefit of learning and practising a craft, the plan was that they might earn a livelihood, using the skills Harold taught them, when they returned home. Their illness made it impossible for them to take up their traditional hunting and trapping again. One of the patients was Kenojuak, who became one of the most successful Inuit artists in the world. Harold also ran a gift shop, selling what they had produced, and maintained a banking system for them. Some had quite healthy accounts when they returned to the north.

In addition to his weekday work with the patients, Harold spent some weekends modelling a portrait of one of them, a young boy named Illya.

"One of the youngsters, Illya of Cape Dorset, an "up" patient, had become my shadow as I went around to the wards. He was a mischievous lad with an infectious smile, so I asked him to pose for me. The process of portrait sculpting was quite a revelation to the patients, who used to come and watch me work. When the features of the boy became a likeness in the soft clay, this quite intrigued my attentive viewers. A couple of years after this, I asked an Inuit lady in Pangnirtung to make me a short jacket (a bum freezer) out of sealskin. When it was delivered I found she had embroidered the syllabics for *Agaminut Niakolioti* ⊲ᑕᒪ₅ᷢ ᓂᐊᐦᖃᓕᐅᐟᏆ in the lining. From then on, I was always known as Agaminut Niakolioti, "the man who makes heads with his hands." This name followed me across the arctic."

A year later, he went to the Arctic as a crafts specialist with the Department of Northern Affairs, and executed four native portraits in bronze. His subjects, especially the old, show their character in their faces; their trials and tribulations, their happiness and sadness. The experience of going out every day to hunt and fish in a place where you either succeed or starve can mark you deeply, and Harold was drawn to that. His craft teaching was a full-time job, so the portraits were all done in his spare time.

His first arctic encounter with the Inuit was while travelling north that summer of 1955 on the icebreaker *C.D. Howe*. There were twelve returning on the ship, going home after their hospital stays. Along with his other work, Harold was a liaison officer, and looked after their baggage, and was generally helpful when questions arose.

Tye of Cape Dorset, Baffin Island, 1954

"When it was not too cold, I frequently stood in the prow, bundled up, hanging on as the ship ploughed into and over a great wall of ice. Sometimes the ice was seven or eight feet thick, but the weight of the ship usually crushed it and pushed great sheets aside. If it did not, the captain reversed the engines and attacked it again and again. Every so often the helicopter took off with a roar on reconnoitring flights and returned with news of possible leads in the ice. The sight of the bright sun on the great chunks of ice as they were mauled and broken was unforgettable."

The trip up the straits, in very dense ice conditions, was extremely slow. Time hung heavily on everyone's hands; the Inuit, especially, were anxious to get home. As a diversion, Harold asked one of the girls to sit while he did a portrait head of her. She was Tye of Lake Harbour, Baffin Island. Her high cheekbones and almond eyes particularly attracted him. Her features were very similar to those of the Yuits whom Harold

Walter Pfeiffer's posters
for tubercular Inuit patients

saw many years later in Siberia. She was painfully shy, but as Harold had known her for a long time, there was an empathy between them. It was a good likeness, and everyone was diverted by the process.

While they were still on board, he cast the head in plaster. One day, when the ship gave a sudden lurch, it fell off the upper bunk in his cabin and the rear half was irreparably damaged.

"When I got home, I sawed the damaged half off, making a mask. It almost looked better than the full head, and I had it cast in bronze. The limited edition of eight sold very quickly. As the saying goes, "It's an ill wind...""

Eventually Harold arrived at Port Harrison (now Inukjuak) on the east shore of Hudson's Bay. It is in the subarctic, and in a good year summer may last almost three months. He was able to indulge in one of his favourite sports, fly-fishing for arctic char, and it was here that he had his first introduction to the kayak, in the form of a very tippy one-seater that leaked badly.

"We were invited across the river to the RCMP camp for an evening party. I had been fishing with Doug Taite, the new assistant manager at The Bay, and we were having such a good time that we came home late and we missed the boat. There were four kayaks sitting up on stone columns out of reach of the dogs, who were always hungry and would eat the skin coverings if they could get to them. Doug took the first one, and I carried another down to the water, wriggled my way into it and started paddling. It was treach-erously tippy, and I struggled to get my balance and paddle in a steady rhythm. About half way across, I found my derrière and other precious parts were absolutely freezing. I felt down my pantleg and discovered my kayak had four inches of water in it. Scared stiff, I yelled to Doug that I was sinking. He shouted back, "Paddle like hell, you're halfway there!" and continued towards the far shore. I finally arrived, soaked to the skin and desperately cold.

"I later learned that a kayak that has been out of the water for any length of time has to be allowed time to soak to seal the seams of the skins. The policemen offered me dry clothing, and I joined the party dressed in a smart pair of navy trousers with a gold stripe down the sides!"

Harold's task was to manage the rehabilitation programme for Inuit returning to the north after treatment. For the first time, he saw some of the men stone carving, and as the stone had to be imported and was often in short supply, he suggested they use caribou antler as an alternative. They carved beautiful little seals, bears, birds and walrus out of the boney material.

"I went on long hikes with some of the younger Inuit, looking for signs of older settlements; stone tent rings from centuries ago, when their ancestors moved about the region from one good hunting or fishing site to another. I was always on the alert for archaeological artifacts from long-abandoned campsites. On a rare occasion, I came across an ancient grave. Because of the permafrost, it was almost impossible to dig graves, so the custom was to wrap the corpse in caribou skins, place it on the ground,

and cover it with rocks. This prevented the foxes and other animals eating the body. Many of the deceased's personal belongings, tools, harpoon heads, ulus or fish-hooks, were wrapped up alongside him. Over the years, storms and strong winds and curious animals sometimes dislodged the rocks and many of these items, carved out of walrus tusk, were scattered. There was a law against desecrating gravesites, prescribing a heavy penalty for violators."

Harold's stay in Inukjuak helped prepare him for the more isolated and undeveloped places he eventually visited and worked in. He completed his four portraits and returned satisfied with his adventures.

Every year the federal government sent a medical X-ray survey team to all arctic settlements to examine everyone for signs of illness, especially tuberculosis, the most prevalent disease in the arctic during the 1950s. The team consisted of a general practitioner, an ear, eye, nose and throat specialist, a dentist, a lung specialist, a nurse and an X-ray technician. In 1955 Harold went with the team; he had been transferred from Port Harrison to the Charles Camsell Hospital in Edmonton, again doing occupational therapy with the Inuit patients. He had had some experience with X-ray equipment during his

Ooah (third from left) at a school dance, Frobisher Bay, 1955 work as a wartime munitions inspector, and when he heard about the trip, he made sure he was included.

These trips were always planned for a time when the majority of the people were in their home settlements, in this case to coincide with Easter. Most of the people who might ordinarily be out on their trap lines or hunting or sealing would be coming home for the festivities. They also knew that they could expect the doctors to be visiting them. It was often a very sad time for those who had to be taken out to the south because of tuberculosis or for some other ailment which could not be treated in the settlement.

"Looking back, I do not know when I worked so hard as on those trips. One had to cover a whole year's activities in a few hours or perhaps a day in each settlement. However, the experience was worth a million and the time passed all too quickly."

In Spence Bay they set up their equipment in the Anglican rectory. There were very few suitable buildings and this appeared to be the most accommodating. The room in which Harold worked was the common room, devoid of furniture except for three long

Harold and Doug Tait in kayaks, Port Harrison (Inukjuak), 1954

benches along the walls. Most of the missionaries provided such a room, which was used for showing slides and movies and for small gatherings. It was always open to anyone to come in and visit the missionary or just to get warm. High on the walls were some children's art work, some religious prints and maxims in syllabics.

"One of my jobs was to call out the names of people as they were wanted in the next room to be X-rayed and examined by the doctors or dentist. My work was almost useless because of my pronunciation of the Inuit names. As I called them out, there were gales of laughter. When they had first names I had a bit of a chance, for most of them were taken from the Bible: Mary, Martha, Mattusee, Markussie, Luccassee, Johanasee, Simonee. The people with those names could usually recognize my pronunciation and try to make out the other name which went with it. It became a bit of a game and they all got lots of fun out of my embarrassment."

Every space was taken on the benches and quite a few squatted on the floor. As is common in the Arctic winter, most of them had a cough of some sort and they had tin cans or pieces of paper in front of them to spit into. One of the most rugged-looking men in the room sat next to the door which opened on to the porch. His name was Kingmitiak. He didn't bother to use a tin, he just opened the door and let go. Sitting alongside him was his wife, who was a few years his senior.

"She had on a *koliktak* (coat) and when she stood up and turned around to collect her mitts on the bench, I was intrigued by the unusual decoration on the back. She had sewn on thin strips of fur, allowing them to hang loosely, cascading down the back. They were probably tails of the *sicsic,* the ground squirrel or maybe mink tails. After Kingmitiak and his wife had been examined and were leaving, I followed them and took photographs of them facing me and then asked them to turn around so that I could get pictures of the back of her koliktak. I guess they thought I was a bit daft and they chuckled a lot about it."

The survey team had hoped to get through with the settlement much earlier, but so many people required immediate treatment they had to spend the night there. As Harold was the thinnest one in the party, he was allotted a space on the floor next to the kitchen stove. The house was sparsely furnished; Canon Whitbread, being a bachelor at the time, didn't object to being without some of the amenities a wife might have insisted upon.

The canon was not really prepared to serve seven extra hungry people, but he had the carcass of a recently killed frozen polar bear in the porch. He cubed a large portion and made a stew of it.

"Even though it was cut into very small cubes, no matter how I chewed it, it did not diminish; in fact, it seemed to double in size and I had to discard the sinewy meat. I was so hungry that I swallowed all my turnips! My distaste for the polar bear meat was heightened when I realized that Kingmitiak had been expectorating on the carcass all the previous afternoon. Actually, I arranged to buy the hide of the bear at The Bay and it became quite a conversation piece in my collection. It was stolen out of my house while I was having some repairs done in winter of 1996."

Thirteen years later, Harold returned to Spence Bay with an assignment to execute a number of Inuit portraits, and as so often happened, everyone remembered him.

"Kingmitiak was quite dramatic upon meeting me again and he told all the others about my taking a lot of photographs of him and his wife. My great regret was that I just could not learn the language and everything had to be interpreted. Conversation always loses its punch in translation. My form of art was completely foreign to the natives and so I figured that perhaps it would be a good idea if I let them see me at work before I had any of them pose for me. I asked Nigel Wilford, the missionary, if he would sit for me. The rectory was exactly as it was when I stayed there thirteen years before. While I worked, many of the natives came in, mostly out of curiosity. Kingmitiak was a frequent visitor and when the bust was finished, he said, "Now we have two Gods!" Needless to say, he became my next sitter. He was a Netsilik and had quite a sense of humour. I was quite taken with his very rugged features; high cheekbones and thick lower lip, and, unusual for an Inuk, a moustache and sideburns.

"When we agreed that I sculpt his head, I suggested that I do it at his little house down by the shore. This was out of sympathy for him, for he was badly afflicted with arthritis and had to support himself with crutches. However, he insisted that he would walk up to the rectory for the sittings. It was early June and the snow was getting very soft. It used to hurt me to see him plodding along, his crutches often sinking deep into the snow. I think it was the tea and biscuits I always gave him that were the attraction. While posing, he chatted a lot, and I wished I had a tape recorder handy so I could find out later what he was saying. His wonderfully rugged head in bronze is in the Glenbow Museum in Calgary."

David Komoyuk personifies the unassuming, good-natured courage of the Inuit that Harold so admires. Harold met him in 1955 when he arrived to join the staff of the Charles Camsell Hospital in Edmonton. When David was about seventeen he lived on the east coast of Victoria Island in a tiny settlement called Cresswell Bay near Ross's Inlet. The winter that year was an exceptionally cold one. There was a scarcity of game; no caribou, seals or walrus and practically no birds. Communication had been cut off because the batteries on their radio phone were dead, preventing their usual scheduled talks with the police in Cambridge Bay. The police made an annual winter visit by dog team to each of the settlements and would eventually go up to Cresswell Bay.

Meanwhile, famine struck deep. They ate all but three of their dogs. They resorted to chewing their mukluks and fur hides—anything to get some nourishment. They had no blubber to make oil for their stoves, so they had no heat and were all but frozen. A long-dead walrus washed up on shore and, ravenous as they were, they ate parts of it. The carcass was poisoned by the lead bullets and harpoon wounds in it and they all

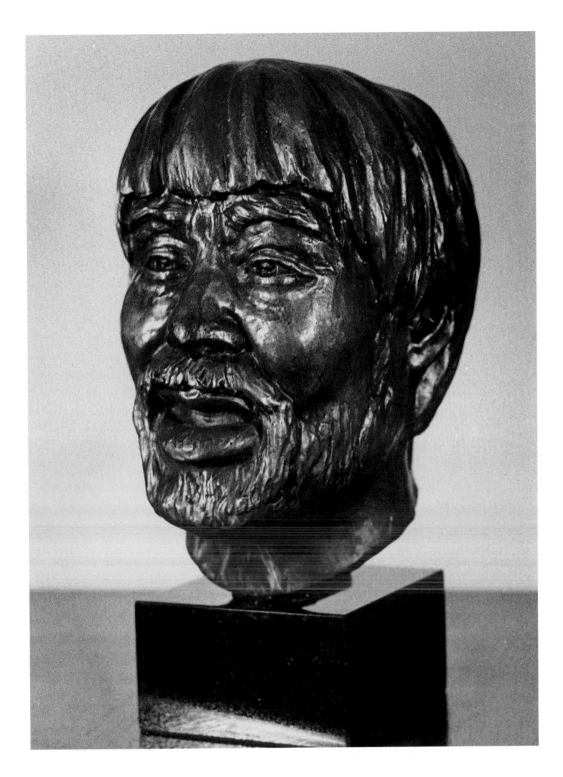

43

Kingmitiak, Spence Bay, NWT, 1968

got dysentery and acute toxic reactions. Only David, his mother and one man, Idlout, survived. Idlout, though he was very ill, harnessed up the three remaining half-starved dogs and left for the nearest settlement, Cambridge Bay. When the desperate foursome arrived the police immediately flew up to save David and his mother.

In the meantime, David's feet had frozen and he got gangrene in both legs. Knowing his condition would soon kill him if they did not act, his mother cut off one of his legs and the next day David cut off the other. A more traumatic situation would be difficult to imagine. As soon as the police arrived they wrapped them up and flew them to Cambridge Bay, and then on to Edmonton. David's mother died. David had an extraordinarily strong constitution and he survived.

His disposition endeared him to all the staff. When he was well enough to have prosthetic legs fitted, he applied himself to relearning how to walk. They had him hold on to the push-bar of a meal wagon as a supporting walker, and he was soon helping deliver meals around the hospital. David learned English and made himself useful, interpreting and assisting with treatment routines. After he was able to walk he was hired as an orderly, and worked there for months. When he felt that he was sufficiently mended and wished to return north, he left. He had been at the hospital for three years. Since all his relatives and friends had died or moved away from Ross's Inlet, and there were no roads there on which he could walk, he settled in Cambridge Bay where there were several paved roads and walking was easier for him.

David had had no expenses while at the hospital and left with a healthy bank balance. He had always wanted to have a dog team and a trapline and now he was in a position to buy them. With quite remarkable optimism he fulfilled his ambition, though after his first winter on his own, he found that attending to his dog team and the trapline was really too much for him and he purchased a snowmobile to replace the dogs. During this time he also married and began fathering a family.

"Several years later, when I was in Cambridge Bay, he took me for a ride on his snowmobile. The next time I was there, enquiring about him, I learned that he had taken a job as a fishing guide at an exclusive camp. The American fisherman liked to lay bets on who could stand in the icy water in hip waders the longest. David amazed them with his endurance. They had no idea he had artificial limbs, and couldn't feel a thing."

"When he was in hospital I asked David if he would carve a polar bear and a seal for me. Although he had not been carving, he got some stone and carved both animals, anatomically perfect, although he had not seen examples of either in over three years. The Inuit have an uncanny gift of observation.

"David's is an epic story and legend has inspired many storytellers to embroider it considerably. I checked this account with him and he assured me that it is accurate. His bronze bust is in the Glenbow Museum in Calgary."

45

David Komoyuk, Cambridge Bay, NWT, 1955

At the end of 1956, Harold arrived to spend a full winter at Apex, near Frobisher Bay (Iqaluit), Baffin Island, experiencing the extreme cold and darkness of the arctic winter for the first time.

"My winter in Apex was not especially exciting, except that I learned to appreciate what really cold weather, minus 30 to 50 degrees fahrenheit, is like. I feel great admiration for the natives who every year experienced the long, dark, dismal days, facing storms, blizzards and high winds in a daily battle for survival."

The house allotted to Harold was poorly built, and during heavy snowstorms, little piles of snow leaked in beneath the windows and in the corners. He boarded up the corners and filled the triangular spaces with sawdust, which helped a bit. Later, when the snow packed hard enough, he built a wall of snow blocks around the house, up to the windows. From then on, while sitting and reading, he did not have to keep his feet on a folded blanket on the floor, or on the open oven door.

For a gregarious type like Harold, this was not the ideal place. The most fun he had was when he was invited over to the nearby DEW line site to the officers mess for a party. The following week, they would all come over to Apex for a return visit. Many of them were Americans, and some showed an interest in art.

"I discovered three chaps from the DEW line post who were interested in my work. I invited them over on a Sunday, and they brought me fresh oranges and apples.

Polar bear, soapstone, carved by David Komoyuk, 1955

They arrived about 11:00 AM and spent the day with me. They were all over 6' 3"; a Canadian, a Scot and an Englishman, and they seemed to fill my little house to bursting. All were well educated and conversation was never lacking. They took over and made lunch and supper from my year's supply of canned food, augmented by goodies they brought with them. This became a weekly event and was a wonderful relief for the four of us. I was beginning to get "bushed," and their cramped quarters were not very pleasant, so they were glad to get out and visit mine, and I looked forward to their visits with much anticipation. I have since visited John Odams at his home in England three times."

Heating the little 612 (612-square-foot house) was a continual challenge. The stove's oil tank had to be filled twice a day, and on very cold days, three times. He had to carry the five-gallon can out to the tank, poke the flashlight into a snowbank and focus it on the tap in the oildrum, bash the tap with a pair of pliers and then tip up the almost empty forty-five-gallon drum to drain out the last of the oil, unscrew the tap opening in a fresh barrel, insert the tap, roll the drum over, bash open the air hole — all while a snowstorm howled around him. There always seemed to be a high wind; there were no trees or buildings to break or deflect it. Even with the stove on full, most of the heat seemed to go up the chimney. This was a hard life for a hot-house city slicker like Harold Pfeiffer, but it was a great experience to look back on.

He found the darkness especially distressing. In December the lamps were on until 10:30 or 11:00 AM, then lit again at about 2:30 PM. On very stormy days the light was on all the time. It was small consolation to remember a parting gift from a friend in Lévis, Quebec: "He handed me a piece of coarse burlap and told me to stroke it every day, saying 'When it starts to feel like velvet, come out immediately.'"

At one point, after a three-day storm which kept him virtually housebound, Harold got so desperately lonely that he decided to walk the three miles to Frobisher to visit with a friend who was passing through. The shorter route was on the shore ice, but it was very rough going; the ice was heaved up in towering blocks, and it was hard work finding a path through them. There had also been several polar bear sightings near shore, so Harold took the road. Halfway there, he realized it was colder than anything he had previously experienced and he was having difficulty breathing. No-one knew where he was, it was just as far to go back as to go on; he began to fear for his life. When he finally arrived at the first building in Frobisher Bay, the RCMP post, he could barely crawl up the steps and bang on the door. The policeman who let him in told him it was minus 51 degrees fahrenheit, and that he was crazy to be out in it.

When he arrived in Apex word of Harold's presence quickly spread around the settlement. Many of the patients he had worked with at the hospital in Quebec City were from this area, and within an hour or so of his arrival, he had met several old friends.

Letia was one of them. While Harold was modelling young Illya's portrait at the hospital, she was always on hand, following his progress. She had told her husband Josee all about it, and the day after Harold's arrival, she brought him in.

"I was immediately attracted by Josee's rugged features. His high cheekbones, pushing his eyes up slightly on the outer corners, are characteristic of his Mongolian ancestors. He had a very prominent lower lip, a usual trait in Inuit men, but in his case, it was exaggerated by a slight facial paralysis. I had made up my mind that here was a man I certainly would like to sculpt and after a while, when I got settled in, I had him pose for me."

As is the custom when visitors come into a house, tent or igloo, tea is immediately brewed and a "mug-up" is offered to the guests, a practice which Harold always followed. In many homes the tea pot is always on the stove, and another scoop of tea is simply tossed into the brew.

Josee had odd jobs around the settlement, keeping him out of doors much of the time. On his arrival for sittings, he would immediately try to thaw his hands by the stove and when Harold handed him a mug of piping hot tea, he would place both hands around it, cradling the mug, warming his hands, always posing in this position.

"When I had just about completed modelling his head, surrounded by the thick fur collar of his attigi, one of the RCMP officers came and asked if he could take photographs of me working on the bust. He was a keen photographer and did a

48

Josee, Warming Hands, Frobisher Bay, Baffin Island, 1956

the forearms, hands and mug. This dramatically described the intense arctic cold. With this addition the grouping turned out to be one of my most successful and prized works. If my collection is ever taken over by a museum or gallery, or if I am forced to live in a small place, I would keep Josee for myself."

Ooah was a woman of considerable importance in the community, the wife of Paulussie, the catechist. Her grandson Simonee was one of the patients at the Hôpital du Parc Savard while Harold was there. He showed considerable interest in crafts and Harold got him doing some stone and wood carving. After he was cured of T.B. he returned to Iqaluit and got a job there. When Harold was transferred to Apex he was one of the first to welcome him.

"He was very anxious to have me meet his grandparents. We became good friends and they more or less adopted me. I decided to sculpt her portrait, so I drove the Land-Rover over every Saturday morning and brought her back to my house for lunch and we would have a long sitting in the afternoon. Inuit rarely travel alone and never object if children decided to come along. The car was always laden with children and their friends. I always provided lunch and none of them had bird-like appetites."

"Ooah did not speak English so the older youngsters had to do the translating. Inuit enjoy a hearty laugh and although much of her conversation did not "get through" to me, we always had a jolly time. Happily there was an empathy between us from the start and it was not essential that we talk.

"Besides being a good family woman, Ooah was very mindful of church activities, but this did not prevent her attending all the social functions of the community. At the dances she was always surroundedby a coterie of young people who thoroughly enjoyed her witticisms and were kept in gales of laughter. When important visitors from the outside came, Ooah was the First Lady of the settlement and was always presented to them.

"I did her portrait in 1956; she passed away in the fall of 1972. The bronze of her is in the Prince of Wales Northern Heritage Centre in Yellowknife."

Elizabee, Port Harrison (Inukjuak), 1954

was the First Lady of the settlement and was always presented to them.
"I did her portrait in 1956; she passed away in the fall of 1972. The bronze of
her is in the Prince of Wales Northern Heritage Centre in Yellowknife."

Harold's paid work in Apex was craft instruction. He did the portraits in his spare
time, just as he did in Port Harrison. He encouraged many of the natives to do stone
carving, with some success; the Hudson's Bay shop purchased all the carvings. He had
some of the women make rag dolls, which they did beautifully, producing
many works of museum quality, decorated with beads, and there was a continual
demand for them.

Harold at the Camsell
Hospital, 1955

50

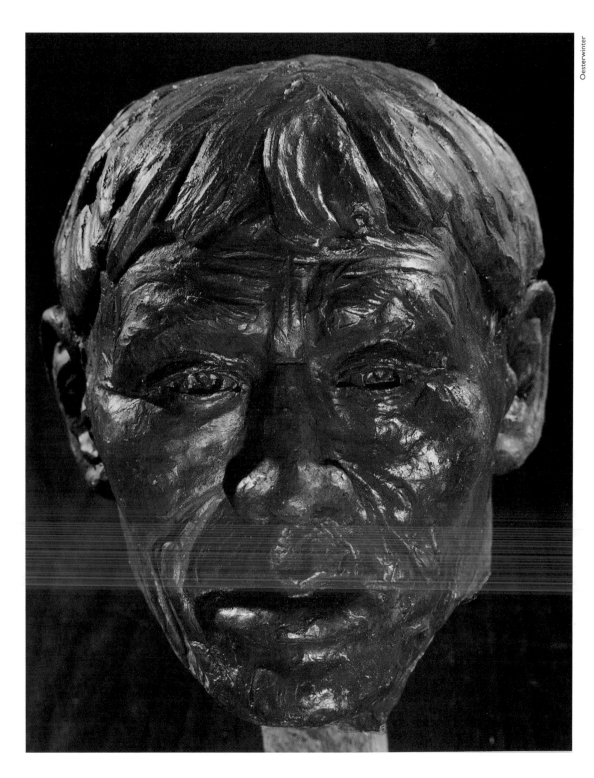

51

Old Willya, Port Harrison (Inukjuak), 1954

Leo Ciceri, Shakespearian actor, 1970

The Museum Years, 1956-1970

n 1956 Harold went to work at the National Museum of Man, now the Museum of Civilization. His first work was as chief cataloguer for the Ethnology Department where he handled, measured and closely studied thousands of artifacts and specimens in the vast collection.

Often, objects came to him which needed to be researched, so that he could properly identify them and their origins, and the materials and methods of their making. The scientists on the museum's staff provided information and directed him to available books on the subject. He thoroughly enjoyed this work, and met many prominent archaeologists and anthropologists who came to study the collections. He was also delighted to be asked to organize and assemble artifacts for displays and exhibitions, sometimes for other museums. In many ways, the job was a perfect marriage of his love of antiquities and his skills as a designer/decorator.

The museum decided to have a birchbark voyageur canoe built, and Harold was assigned the job of overseeing its construction. It was to be constructed as authentically as possible, using the traditional materials. The actual building of the canoe was under the direction of Chief Bernard of Rice Lake. Arrangements had to be made to find trees large enough to yield the very large birchbark needed, and transportation to the museum was a challenge because of the canoe's size. It was the major display on the main floor of the museum for many years.

In 1957 Harold organized an Irish folklore exhibition, entitled Irish Yesterdays. This was to have consisted only of enlarged photographs of early Celtic designs from churches and grave stones and from historic ruins in Ireland. They were beautiful, but he felt that the show could have more impact and persuaded the director to allow him to borrow some artifacts from other sources to enrich the displays. He had friends at the Metropolitan Museum in New York and persuaded them to loan a few items, something they had never done before.

"It must have been my Irish charm, for they let me have a fine collection of very old Waterford crystal and a very old harp. I could hardly contain my happiness about this. From St. Michael's College in Toronto I borrowed a very valuable replica of a 12th century chalice which was decorated with many precious stones, delicate cloisonné and enamels. The Irish Ambassador, Mr. T.J. Kiernan, loaned us another precious item, a replica of the ancient Book of Kells. As an added attraction, I organized an evening of classical Irish song and dance with Tom Kines as our featured singer. It was quite a superior concert. *Does yer Mother Come From Oireland?* was not on the program."

Probably the most prestigious exhibition Harold arranged was The West Coast Indian Exhibition which was held in Stratford, Ontario in 1960, during the Shakespearean Festival. He was responsible for the design and layout of the whole exhibition. He even designed the special security cases in which the artifacts were shown and the special lighting for the masks and ceremonial blankets. The exhibition was a lavish celebration of the artistic wealth of West Coast native culture. Along with the displays of ancient artifacts, a Haida carver, Mrs. Ellen Neel from Skidegate, Queen Charlotte Islands, carved a large totem pole with the help of her husband, Ted. The exhibition was a knock-out, crowded with spectators most of the time.

"An added dividend for me was that one of my favourite plays, *A Midsummer Night's Dream,* was on most of the summer and I was a guest at five performances. My actor friend, Leo Ciceri, introduced me to all his theatrical friends. We had known each other for years. I followed his career from his start in Montreal with several play groups, including the Montreal Repertory Theatre, through his many successes at Stratford from 1961 until Leo was killed in a tragic motor car accident in Stratford in 1970. I was subsequently commissioned to do his bust for the theatre. It is on display in the lobby of the Festival Theatre."

In 1960, the Historical Division was established at the Museum of Man, with a mandate to develop a representative collection of Canadiana. At the time, there were no properly qualified people on the staff of the museum to head the division. However, Dr. Russell, the Museum Director, knew of Harold Pfeiffer's knowledge of antiques, his collecting experience on Dr. Barbeau's behalf, and that he had studied at the Victoria and Albert Museum in London and at the Louvre, and so he appointed him custodian. The work consisted of completing the cataloging of the existing collection, and scouring the country for more. "I went to every junk shop, antique store and garage sale in the country. Friends would call up and say, 'My Great-Aunt So-and-So has a shed full of old junk. You should go out and see her.' And off I'd go."

During his time at the museum, Harold travelled when he could, and slowly built up his collection of native portraits during holidays and in his spare time. In 1960 he made a trip to Newfoundland for three months to collect artifacts from the island's early history for the museum's collections. He was given a miserly purchasing budget of $500.

"Newfoundland is an immense province, and I had no idea where to start my collecting tour. Our librarian, Audrey Dawe, a Newfoundlander, gave me the name of a man who could put me on the right track. He was Nimshi Crewe, a historian and scholar, and a friend of Premier Joey Smallwood.

"The first person I looked up was Leslie Tuck, an ornithologist whom I had met when he was fogged in at Apex in 1956. I had an extra bedroom, so he stayed with me for a week. We got along famously, and he did all the cooking!"

Tuck lived in St. John's and he took a few days off to show Harold around the Avalon Peninsula in his car. Before he left on an expedition to study murres in the arctic, he gave Harold the use of a large basement room in the Sir Humphrey Gilbert Building to store the material he hoped to collect.

Harold first visited the antique shops of St. John's, but he found nothing of interest that fit his modest budget. When Harold called him for advice about good collecting sites, Nimshi Crewe invited him to his home for Sunday dinner. The house was filled with exceptionally fine antiques, and he seemed pleased that Harold was knowledgable about them. The meeting was most instructive. Another guest there was Mr. Don Andrews, visiting from Jamaica, who used to live in Port de Grave on Conception Bay.

After he had described his mission, both suggested he start looking for artifacts in Port de Grave. It sounded like an ideal spot because there were six other potentially interesting villages within walking distance, and Harold had no car. They were amused when he asked what hotel he could stay at; there was no such thing in any of those fishing villages. Don said he had some relatives with a large house, who might take in a boarder for a few days until he got established. In the end, he stayed with them for six weeks.

It turned out Don's nephew had a car, and was the community taxi driver. When he had a call some distance away, he would take Harold along and drop him off. Later on, if he was passing by without a passenger, he would pick him up again. When he collected heavy objects, he would get a truck and drive them to St. John's, where Harold deposited his treasures in the room Les Tuck had loaned him.

The first two days were very disappointing. The first thing he did was change his city clothes for casual ones and walk to the general store. The people on the road took shy glances at him, the foreigner from Canada.

Albert Porter,
Port de Grave,
Newfoundland, 1960

56

"In the store, I ambled over to a group of young men around the jukebox. When I tried conversation, they looked suspicious and answered in monosyllables. Discouraged, I wandered down to the wharf where the boats were disgorging their cargos of cod. On the upper level of the wharf women were standing at a table cutting up the fish and throwing the livers into barrels and the entrails into the sea. The fish went into low wooden tubs. As I stood, a fascinated landlubber, watching this procedure, I spotted three old fishermen sitting on a bench, and I went over to join them. The awful stench of rendering cod liver permeated everything.

"They acknowledged me with a low 'ah-hum' as I sat down beside them. The man next to me said, ''n what be you doin' here?' I told him I was from Ottawa and interested in collecting very old artifacts for our museum. I learned very soon that 'Ottawa' was a dirty word around many parts of the island and I only mentioned it when I had to. I asked if they had anything which they might like to sell me, such as old flintlock rifles, sealing rifles, powder horns, etc. One fellow said he had an old horn. Could I see it? 'Yas, cum up after supper, me house has the red shutters, third one up the road.' What time would be good? 'Six o'clock.'

"I arrived on the dot. Everyone was in the kitchen. Several men were 'talking cod' and continued for at least half an hour before they sort of noticed me and

I asked about the powder horn. 'Billy, Billy boy, be a gud un and git the powder hern up in the laft.' Billy returned with a most miserable example hardly more than six inches long. I looked it over and asked how much he would want for it and he said it was not much of a one but would not come up with a price. I suggested three dollars and he immediately agreed. I thought, at least I have my foot in the door.

"When I got home, my host was astonished the fellow had had the gall to take three dollars for it. He asked me if they had shown me the pair of duelling pistols in the fancy box or the fine grandfather clock with the wooden works or the desk with the secret drawers. I was crestfallen. They had not shown me anything but the powder horn.

"The next day, the welcome along the roadway was just as cold as on the first day. I decided I would have to change my approach. Before I left Ottawa, Dr. Russell had told me that the elements were frequently unkind down on the island. 'Sometimes the fog will roll in on you for a whole week or more; perhaps you should bring along some clay and maybe model an old fisherman.' God love him!

"That afternoon I noticed, on a bit of a knoll by the sea, directly opposite my digs, three old men sitting, chewing tobacco and spitting. I watched them for a while, and noticed that one of them always turned when a truck or car went by and shouted out a greeting. He obviously knew everyone in the village and seemed to be a popular and gregarious fellow.

I made up my mind then and there that a fog was definitely rolling in! I sauntered over and sat with the men. ''n what be ya doin' here?' I made no mention of Ottawa or the museum: I said that I was an artist. 'Not one of them painter fellas ya sees around these parts?' one of them asked .

"'No, I am a sculptor.' I drew several photos out of my wallet showing some of my bronze portraits, one showing me with the sitter alongside the clay model, which really resembled him.

"'You done them? Bejeez, it's his spitten image!' They devoured the photos and were quite amazed. The garrulous one had an interesting face; the deep-set eyes of a seaman, no teeth, cavernous cheeks. Asking him leading questions about his past, I got a rundown of his life story: 'When oi were a gaffer of thirteen, oi went fishin wit me fadder in his boat an only gived up a few years past.' I said his face told quite a story, and I would like to hear some of his fishing stories while I was around.

It was an opportunity I could not miss, so I said, 'You have great features; the history of Newfoundland is written there. I'd really like to do a bust of you.' I told him what would be required on his part and that when I was finished, I would give him some money for his time. He hemmed and hawed until one of his pals said, "Go arn Al, ya sit fer the fella," and it was arranged. My sitter's name was Al Porter.

Cauldron for barking nets,
Twillingate, Newfoundland, 1960

"My hosts, the Andrews, had an old single car garage just below the house on the side of the road. The twin doors opened directly onto the gravel road. They said I could use it for my studio. I found some old crates, built an armature and set up directly in front so as to get lots of light and also so that passers-by could not help seeing me modelling.

"When Al's features started to come through, during the second sitting, I noticed many passers-by took a quick peek, and then seemed to have forgotten something at the store, and so had to pass a second time. When Al was there, he always had something to say to them. Word got around about 'the fella doin' Al Porter's pitur,' and in the evening after supper there were truckloads of people with all the kids coming to see me work. That far north, the daylight was with us a long time, and I took advantage of it.

"I timed my sittings and frequently prolonged them so that as many people as possible could see what I was doing. In the meantime, my host had phoned several friends about my real mission, and arranged for me to visit houses that might have something of interest. Things were brightening up for me.

"I also did some foraging on my own. Near one of the old cooperages that used to make wooden barrels in vast quantities for the salt cod trade, I found a creek bank that had been used as a depository for discards from the works. Leaning over the rail of the bridge, I spotted several old rusty planes lying amongst a lot of other metal discards. I rummaged around, and brought back an armful of odds and ends. Some I could not identify. I cleaned them up a bit, and placed them on the workbench in my 'studio.' When the curious came to see me work, I would get up and point out an object which puzzled me and ask what it was.

"One, for instance, was a long narrow loop of iron with three iron rings on it. 'Oh, thet's a fish trouncer; ya drap thet overboard to the bottom an' clang it a few toimes. The fish get scart 'n rise to the top an' we gets them in our nets.' Sometimes I would pick up something else whose use was quite unknown to landlubbers, and giving me its name, they would say, 'Thet's jest groat (rubbish); we's got a better one. Come up and have a pick (meal) with us 'n' we'll show yer some t'ings.' After a bit, realizing I was not as green as I was cabbage-looking, they came to accept me.

"On several occasions a fisherman would just set me loose to rummage around in the loft of his fish house by the shore. If it was near lunch time, he and his family would ask me in to share their meal, which was usually fish and brewis, which is made from salt cod and hard tack, or turnips and salt cod.

"I found the Newfoundland dialect endlessly fascinating. One young lad came by, looking quite miserable, and I asked him what was wrong. "Oi got an awful bad pain in me hornspike 'n oi kint glutch," he said, meaning he had a sore throat and couldn't swallow.

"News got around about my sculpting and a reporter came out from a St. John's newspaper to interview me. He was a cub reporter and the first thing he said was that he had never done anything on art and would I help him write up something; he just handed it to me on a platter.

"Yes, I wrote most of the article, saying I found the island very interesting and the sea-coast fascinating. I mentioned a few of the more unusual articles which I had collected, many of which the younger folk had never seen or heard of. It was a great joy to me that so many people had opened up their fish houses for me to explore on my own. Although I was offering payment for everything, frequently people just gave things to me (revealing this may have been my downfall). I was a happy fellow and I just loved Newfoundland.

"For this I got a lot of publicity. Everyone in Newfoundland reads the paper thoroughly. It certainly eased my entry into the other towns and villages I visited later in the trip. I was asked to exhibit Al Porter's bust in a prominent shop in St. John's. The publicity also caught the attention of Premier Smallwood and his henchman, Nimshi Crewe.

"Whenever I went to the city with a load of my "treasures" I phoned Mr. Crewe and told him of my various finds, and asked him to come and help me identify some of them; he would be likely to know what they were. I could not go back to my museum not knowing the identity of the objects in my collection.

"While I was away in the northern islands collecting, quite unknown to me, a key had been found, and certain knowledgeable people came in to look over my finds. I was supposed to have the only key.

"I went to St. John's many times while I was on the island, and, entirely on my own initiative, I decided to pay a courtesy call on the premier. The first time I tried to make an appointment, his secretary told me that Governor-General and Madame Vanier were visiting the island and that Mr. Smallwood would be very busy with them all week. A few weeks later, when I was invited to the Lieutenant-Governor's garden party, I again tried to see him, but he was away at a premiers' conference in Ottawa. The third time, he was up-country laying a cornerstone, so we never got together.

"At the garden party, friends introduced me to Derrick Bowering, of the very old family of merchants and fish traders. Hearing of my work, he suggested that we get together on my next visit to town and he would bring me over to the wharfs where there were many two- and three-hundred-year-old items, just rusting. I was intrigued and said I would take him up on his generous offer.

"I combed all the settlements along the peninsula, going into fish-houses, sheds, attics, root houses, often finding unusual objects. Most people just set me loose to rummage around. After a month or so, I had learned a great deal about the early fishing and sealing industry and various types of rifles, lures and decoys. It was a most fascinating experience.

"On Twillingate Island, I became friendly with Ted Drover, and with that legendary character, Dr. John Olds, of St. Anthony's Grenfell Mission, who had attracted much attention for performing plastic surgery on many young children, especially those who had been dreadfully burned while playing around the huge iron pots the nets were boiled in. The pots were about four feet across and some three feet deep. They were filled with pine and balsam cones and the resin was cooked out of them. The nets were immersed and the resin impregnated them, prolonging their life in the water.

"Dr. Olds was about to go to the outports, making his rounds in the hospital ship, the *Bonnie Nell*. Knowing I was interested in covering as many of the islands as possible in my limited time, he suggested I come along and mosey about looking for interesting specimens while he and his assistant and the nurse attended to the sick.

"In some places we tied up to the wharf, in others, without docking facilities, we anchored and the patients were rowed out to the ship. There was a terrible polio scare at the time, and everyone was receiving Salk vaccine shots. I had never had one, and seeing the nurse administer a shot to almost everyone coming aboard, I decided to have her give me my first shot, and get the booster when I got home.

"The first night on board I stayed out on deck for hours, watching the northern lights. They seemed a mere arm's length away and their movements were fascinating. I got chilled and developed a miserable cold. We sailed on to New Worlds Island, Change Islands and more, and sometimes in the evening, when the Doc had to see some bed patients, I went along with him and shone my flashlight on the affected parts. It was almost a repetition of my experiences on the X-ray survey. Shortly after this trip I began to feel miserable, and on several trips by water-taxi over rough water I was really seasick, which I could not understand; I am normally a very good sailor.

"When we returned to Twillingate, my time and budget had dwindled and my visit had to end. I arranged to have my collection packed and shipped off to Ottawa. This proved to be a good move, though I thought nothing of it at the time. The ferry trip between Twillingate and the main island was always very rough. As I was still feeling miserable I just could not face that terrible ferry ride. A large freighter was in port, and one of the stevedores told me that it would be sailing for St. John's at 6:00 PM. I rushed up the gangway and begged

Cartoon that appeared in the Toronto Star at the conclusion of Harold's collecting trip to Newfoundland (Reidford)

a spot in the lounge from the captain as there were no berths available. I tore back to my digs, said my adieus to all, and was off.

"I spent a pleasant evening chatting with the men, and an uncomfortable night on the couch in the lounge. I sat up in the early morning to accept the cup of tea and biscuits they brought me, and bolted for the rail. I was dreadfully seasick all day long. I felt better when I got on terra firma in St. John's.

"When I got back to the room I had kept in the city, my landlady said, "Oh, Mr. Smallwood has been trying to trace you and he wants you to call him at his farm as soon as you can." Newfoundland friends in Ottawa had told me that Smallwood had a large city house full of fine antiques and a similar country house and several barns full of antiques and other artifacts. They had suggested that perhaps he might like us to have some really fine pieces representing Newfoundland, and either donate them in a fit of generosity or offer some for sale. Wishful thinking!

"I called him on the Sunday before Labour Day and he said he would like to talk to me about something of mutual interest and could I come out to his farm on Monday? I told him I was ill, so he asked me to come to his office on Tuesday.

"I felt much better on Monday, and at Derrick Bowering's suggestion, I arranged to see his wharf manager, Mr. Chesley, I think, who showed me over their vast ancient buildings. I was to have any old things which were not serving a purpose at the moment. I collected a lock which was about 2.5" thick, 10" by 12" with a huge, heavy, intricately designed key; also several old box compasses, some whaling harpoons, one of which was hollow and used to pump air into the whale's carcass so that it would float. The prize was a swivel whaling gun from a vessel called *Thetis*. I purred with happiness. This was the greatest haul of the whole trip and I blessed Mr. Bowering. I took some small items with me in a taxi, saying I would call for the rest the next day.

"At the premier's office at the dot of 10:00 AM I was surprised to find Nimshi Crewe in the waiting room. Mr. Smallwood asked what I was doing on the island. I told him that the National Museum was planning a display representing each of the provinces, and I was sent down to collect artifacts which I felt would describe the early days of fishing, whaling and sealing. 'I am glad to know that Ottawa knows that there is such a place as Newfoundland,' he said sarcastically, 'but what they don't know is that we will not permit any of this material to leave the island.' He then proceeded to give a long dissertation on the depression years when their collection of museum articles had been dispersed to the four winds to make way for British Government offices. To protect their museum's future they had passed an Order-in-Council prohibiting the removal of antiques or historical artifacts from the country. He then had Mr. Crewe read me the law, and I was shocked when Crewe leaned over to me and said that he had drafted the law himself a few years before. Clearly, they had never had any intention of allowing the artifacts off the island, but had simply allowed me to do all the spade work for them.

"Crewe and Professor Fraser of Memorial University, Newfoundland's archivist, were to inspect my collection. They might allow me to take a few small items, or they might not. After working seven days a week, fifteen or more hours a day for three months, in all weather conditions, this was a very traumatic revelation for me. It was also apparent that Mr. Smallwood knew of my visit to the docks on the previous day, because he specifically announced that none of the items I had collected there were to leave the island either."

They kept the majority of the collection. Fortunately, Harold had kept photographs and detailed records of the origin and price of each item. All the items he had collected in the Twillingate area arrived safely in Ottawa, and are now in the Museum of Civilization in Hull.

Feeling mentally and physically wretched (he eventually discovered he was suffering from infectious hepatitis, which laid him up for a year), Harold returned to Ottawa on the first available plane. The press had been informed, and exaggerated and inaccurate reports appeared in the papers. One paper ran a three-inch headline reading 'Smallwood Wins Again.' A Toronto paper ran a long article with a Reidford cartoon of Harold at the 'Newfoundland dig' in safari gear, surrounded by ancient artifacts and signs saying 'King Joey,' and 'Newfoundland Rights,' 'Beware the Curse of Smallwood', 'First Dynasty.'

"I was pretty angry at first," says Harold. "I appreciate the need to protect such artifacts, but I resented the devious way they acquired my treasures. However, my friends got a big kick out of it, and eventually I did, too."

Shortly after Harold retired from the museum in 1970, several of the museum's archaeologists, doing research in St. John's, could not find any trace of the confiscated collection. It is known that officers and others returning to the U.S. from the air base in Quidi Vidi often carried loads of Newfoundlandia with them. In spite of the law, it appears that if the price was right, these artifacts were not prevented from leaving the island.

Elizapee Padlayat, Sugluk, Hudson Straits, 1969

Back to the Arctic and Into the West

1968 was a turning point in Harold Pfeiffer's career. In the year leading up to Expo '67, the Montreal World's Fair that was about to attract millions of visitors from all over the world, few of whom knew anything about Canada's native people, Harold proposed that a special area be set up to display his bronzes of native people, with demonstration areas where natives could do art and craft work, especially Inuit stone carving. The proposal was rejected.

Friends advised him to advance the proposal to various corporations, suggesting that one of them might sponsor such an exhibition. The Riveredge Foundation of Calgary, which established the Glenbow Museum, though it did not take up the Expo proposal, responded with great interest in Harold's native portraits, and the president, Mr. Hod Meech and the secretary, Mr. Fish, came to Ottawa to see them. They purchased eleven bronzes on the spot.

It is important to recognize the validating effect this recognition had on Harold Pfeiffer. Up until this moment, his pursuit of native portraiture had been a private passion, gaining him little recognition in the world, especially in the world of art, which was hypnotized by the fashion for abstraction and had no time for classical realism.

His fellow-workers at the museum thought his dream of a complete circumpolar collection of portraits was simply bizarre. To have an important public institution recognise the value of his work in such a dramatic way turned his life around.

The following year, Riveredge's founder, Mr. Eric Harvie, sent him to the Arctic to sculpt more native people. Harold had said in his proposal that if they paid all travelling

Black Sleep, Blood Reserve, Cardston Alberta, 1955

expenses and a small sum for each head or bust, he would guarantee to do eight to twelve portrait heads. He did eleven and they took all of them. To do this, he took a three month's leave of absence without pay from the National Museum. For many years after this, Riveredge commissioned portraits of Inuit, and Slavey, Blood and Blackfoot Indians as well.

"Mr. Harvie was really my first great benefactor. He commissioned me to sculpt many chiefs and other Indians and Inuit, as well as some of his good friends, such as Governor-General Vanier, Marius Barbeau and Dr. George Gooderham. I first met him at Coste House in Calgary, the headquarters of the

Riveredge Foundation, while I was at the Camsell Hospital in Edmonton in the mid-fifties. The director at the time was Dr. Douglas Leechman, an old friend from the National Museum. We had a dinner engagement and Doug asked me to meet him at Coste House. He had a few things still to do, so he suggested I wander around and look at the endless array of art and artifacts from all over the world.

"Upstairs I came upon a little man unwrapping a collection of jade carvings, trying to find the matching teak bases for them. The first thing I said was, 'I can't understand why the Foundation would purchase items like these. In Toronto's Chinatown you can find better bases.' As we left, Doug advised me I had been talking to Mr. Harvie. What an introduction!"

"Some months later Doug came to Edmonton to see me and the portrait bust I had just completed of Black Sleep, a Blackfoot Indian from Cardston, Alberta. He was very keen on it and suggested I send the plaster casting to Calgary for the Foundation's approval. They weren't interested."

The Glenbow Museum now owns fifty-eight Pfeiffer portraits, including the one of Black Sleep. The agreement between the sculptor and the museum stipulated that Harold deliver the original mould as well as the bronze of each work, so he was unable to make more bronzes for sale to other parties. Copyright rests with the Glenbow Museum.

Finding accommodation in arctic settlements was a problem. Months of letter writing, personal appointments and phone calls were necessary to arrange for a place to stay, a place to eat, how much food to bring, if any, how much working area would be required and how long a time the space would be required. There was little privacy in accommodation and it was impossible to guarantee a private room.

When all arrangements were made for where the sittings were to take place, and when it was understood what time of day the sitting was to be and agreement about it all had been established and repeated, Harold would start building up his armature and work would begin.

"Luckily, in summer there is daylight so much of the time, I could work for sixteen to eighteen hours a day if I wanted to, and many days a week I did just that. Being in the arctic was such a privilege, I wanted to make use of every minute. The Inuit, even if many of them wore wrist-watches, did not worry too much about being on time—I soon learned that. Also, sitting quietly while I worked, they, with their acute hearing, would be alerted to the sound of approaching ducks or geese long before I was aware of them. In a flash, they would be away after a rifle: no by-your-leave, they just bolted. Or they might see a seal's head pop out of the water and in a jiffy, would rush for their rifle and off to the shore or to a handy kayak. On one occasion, I was just catching the likeness of my sitter and he did not turn up for a few days; without telling me, he had promised to help a friend at a camp nearby. Time meant so much to me; I hadn't sufficient clay or plasticine to start another one while he was away. There were many frustrations but I was always so grateful for their angel-perfect immovability when posing."

Realistic portraiture and the process of modelling were still a novelty, and Harold was always surrounded by an audience, especially children. "They would hardly let out a peep; they just whispered comments to one another. Occasionally one of the older ones would break the silence with some comment in Inuktitut which must have been very amusing, for everyone would double up laughing. When the model really resembled the sitter and I was about to call it a day, someone would often place a cigarette or a pipe in the mouth, and then there would be gales of laughter, signalling their acceptance and approval."

Stephen Angulalik and Harold first met in 1955 when Harold went north with the medical X-ray survey party. Stephen was the leader of the settlement at Perry River, which is near Bathurst Inlet on the mainland of the Northwest Territories. The whole settlement came down to meet the plane.

"After landing on the sea ice, when the motors stopped, we stepped off the plane to be greeted by everyone. I particularly remember watching Angulalik. Judging by his aristocratic bearing he was the leader."

The first to descend was Dr. Bill Davies, who was in charge of the party. With much dignity, Stephen approached Dr. Davies and standing erect, bowed from the waist and with a very broad friendly smile, shook hands. In the north, upon meeting, they shake hands with everyone, even to the smallest child peeking out through the fur of his mother's attigi hood. They do not pump the hand as southerners do; they hold it for a moment, then let it go.

"Stephen was dressed in a parka made of caribou with an elaborate but discrete decoration on it. The shoulders had piping of red stroud which was repeated around the edging of an appliqué band around the base of the parka and on the cuffs. These bands were made of tiny geometric oblongs, diamonds and triangles of finely shaved and dyed caribou fur appliquéd on the fur or stroud. The colours were red, black and white. For comparison, I think of the wedding outfit an Inuit girl in Greenland put on for me to admire. Much of her costume was made of bleached pure white caribou but the appliqué was much the same as that on Stephen's parka. The Greenlander's bead-work capes are most beautifully made and are unique to that country.

"The weather was bitterly cold at Perry River and they had a lot of trouble getting the generator going to provide electricity for the X-ray equipment. As I was not mechanically inclined and I was really very cold, I went into the house. Stephen had two wives and the family all lived in the same house and all seemed to be most happy with the arrangement. His wives were very good needlewomen. Stephen's English was almost nil but through our interpreter I asked if he happened to have any old Inuit artifacts which he might like to sell. He produced a box which had some very interesting objects in it. If memory serves me right, there were snow-knives made from antlers, bone snow-beaters, two pairs of ivory scissors with copper edges on the blades, an arrow straightener, quite a few seal and walrus harpoon heads, fish lures and long bone plugs used to stop up the bullet holes in the hides of seal to prevent the blood from flowing out.

"A very old ivory fish lure had a price of fifteen cents on it and alongside it was a similar one made by Stephen priced at perhaps $1.15. It was quite an assortment, with several really old items of considerable value to museums. I was intensely interested in acquiring them and felt that in the long run, the total cost would surely be worth it, so I bought most of them. They are now in the Glenbow Museum. There seemed to be a special empathy between us and later on as we were all saying goodbye, the interpreter came to me and said that Angulalik told him to tell me that we would meet again."

It was fourteen years before they did meet again, this time in Cambridge Bay, Victoria Island, N.W.T. in 1968. Angulalik owned a Peterhead, a sturdy boat like a lifeboat, as well as a schooner in which he collected furs from the natives living along the coast. The Hudson's Bay Company had operated a post in Perry River for many years, but, because of the diminishing fur harvest, the company decided to close up. Angulalik had worked in the post for many years, and was quite familiar with the stock and demands of the natives, and the company asked him if he would take it on. They

69

Stephen Angulalik, Perry River, NWT, 1968

agreed to supply him with merchandise as required. He was very methodical keeping track of the supplies, and by using hunt-and-peck typing, he would send the company the annual inventory and requests for more supplies. He was not really literate, but he was resourceful in working out the spelling of items he wanted to order.

In the intervening years, he had apparently been driven to kill three men. One of these unhappy instances was in 1956-57, at a New Year's Eve party. The victim was a stranger to the community and considerably taller than most of the other men. It was said that when he brought in his furs to trade, he always seemed to have a few more pelts than most of the other trappers. They also noticed that they found their traps empty more often than usual, though there were signs that an animal had been caught. Stealing from another's trapline is an unpardonable violation in the north. He had been warned that he was under suspicion, but the outrage continued. Another serious problem was that this individual was attracted to one of Angulalik's wives and Angulalik was not interested in trading. During the party, the man deliberately bumped into Angulalik on several occasions, making him stumble. This provocation became too much, and Angulalik stabbed him in the stomach. Being quite drunk at the time, the victim slumped where he was and fell asleep. Next morning, he walked home, opening up the wound in his stomach. His bowel escaped, causing a strangulated hernia. He died the next day. Angulalik wrote a full account of the incident to the police, saying that he had not intended killing the man but wanted him to know who was the leader and that his presence in the community was not wanted anymore. Two weeks later, a doctor and a RCMP officer came to investigate and the doctor said that had he used a couple of band-aids over the cut he would have survived. At the trial, Angulalik was acquitted because of provocation.

"As I approached his house, I was astonished to see the chimney was wrapped in caribou skins. I was told that this improved the draft in the chimney in very cold weather, because it kept the flue warmer. Some writers have recorded that Angulalik murdered two other men at the urging of the elders in the community. He was acquitted but was moved away with his family to Cambridge Bay. In sympathy and freindship, the whole community moved to Cambridge Bay with him. Many white people found it difficult to pronounce his name and he was frequently referred to as "Uncle Alex." When I was in Cambridge Bay, I was invited to his home for several dances. He was an excellent drum-dancer. I understand that he descended from the Netsilikmuit. His portrait bust is in the Prince of Wales Northern Heritage Centre in Yellowknife, N.W.T."

Satkatsiak said she was born in the Netsilik Lake area south of Spence Bay, Boothia Peninsula. No dates of birth were recorded in those days, but by listening to her recount events which took place in her earliest memory it was clear to Harold that when he sculpted her portrait bust, she was very old indeed. He was consumed with curiosity to hear her first impressions of white men.

Satrkatsiak, Spence Bay, NWT, 1968

Satkatsiak lived with her granddaughter and her family in a small house set in a field strewn with rocks and pebbles. In the summer, these rocks gleam with damp, giving the appearance of having been oiled. The permafrost melts on the surface and, having nowhere to drain to, there being more permafrost below, water stands in puddles everywhere.

"I only went to her house twice and found the walk quite treacherous. The first time was to discuss the idea of having the old lady pose for me. Knowing how feeble she was, I suggested that I bring all my gear to her house but was most relieved when the family suggested that I work on her at the nearby school house. However, I really shuddered to think of her walking over those slippery rocks twice a day for our sittings. I had seen her walking to a nearby house, all bent over, supported by a cane. A cane was also necessary as protection against dogs which might be on the loose, for should she have fallen, and the dogs in the vicinity were hungry, they certainly would have attacked her. We arranged that a great-granddaughter bring her to the school every afternoon about 1:30 PM.

"As it was June and most of the snow had melted it was still necessary to wear rubber boots. When she arrived at the school porch, she would laboriously pull off her rubber boots and come in in her stocking feet. After sitting for some ten minutes, her heavy eyelids drooped and her head started to fall towards her chest. She would straighten up and give me a grin.

"No words were necessary for there was an empathy between us, as she realized that I knew and appreciated her venerable age. Our sittings were short and I always

72

interrupted them by giving her a mug of tea. While she was more relaxed and dunking biscuits into her mug, I asked her to tell me about her first meeting with white men, through her great-granddaughter, my interpreter."

She had come from what is known today as Back's River, south of the Boothia Peninsula. The rare trapper or hunter who passed by was always an Inuk, speaking the same language and probably a blood relative. They believed that the Inuit, meaning, "the People," were the only people in the world. At that time, the only boats they were familiar with were kayaks and the umiak, a long boat covered with walrus hides.

The people awakened one morning to see a huge umiak anchored in the bay. "It had a house built on it." Panic ran through the settlement and they all rushed up the slope and "made like boulders," hiding among the rocks. "When the white men beached their row boats, we saw men with blond hair, white faces covered with hair and some had beards." Inuits' hair is always jet black and straight and they rarely have facial hair. "One man had red hair and they were dressed so differently from us. They walked along the beach but they didn't have any bows and arrows or harpoons, so we knew they weren't going to kill us so we came down from the hills and met them."

The white men were Scandinavians. This was in 1904-5, when the explorer Amundsen and his crew got caught in the ice in the schooner *Gjoa* and had to spend the winter there.

"Three of the very old people whom I have sculpted told me how frightening it was to see these pale-faced men for the first time, men having 'snow-faces covered with hair.'"

"Of all the Inuit whom I have sculpted, I think that Satkatsiak was undoubtedly the most interesting. I regretted so much that communication with her was so difficult. I think her memory went back over 80 years. Oh, to have talked to her in her own tongue and recorded it on tape! Any of the Inuit who were from this area and born prior to 1904-5 were of the purest stock. None of these people are left today and I was most fortunate in being able to record their likenesses for posterity. Satkatsiak was a woman out of history and may have been the last of the essential Inuit. She died in Spence Bay on May 22, 1970. I did her portrait there in 1968. The bronze of her is in the Prince of Wales Northern Heritage Centre in Yellowknife.

"In 1968, in Pelly Bay, I was fortunate enough to be commissioned by the Glenbow Museum in Calgary to sculpt Zacharie Itimangak. Besides being one of the most respected men in the community, he was a good hunter, fisherman and craftsman and a leader in his own way. The Glenbow Museum had given me carte blanche to purchase items for them which they did not have in their collection. Having seen the quality of many of the items which Itimangak had made, I had him build a kayak, some fish hooks and lures and fish gouges. These replicas were made in the authentic way as his ancestors had done. Some years later, a movie was made of Farley Mowat's book Never Cry Wolf and Itimangak was chosen to play the part of the Inuk who discovered the scientist living on lemmings and mice. After finishing his portrait I also did a high relief of his wife and child. His bust is in the Prince of Wales Northern Heritage Centre in Yellowknife."

It was on this first trip to the arctic for the Riveredge Foundation that Harold met another great benefactor. For thirteen years the Commissioner of the Northwest Territories was Stuart Milton Hodgson. 1968 was the first year of his "reign." Harold was working in Pelly Bay where he had rented a house and had sculpted the heads of seven Inuit in that area. He had run out of plaster of Paris and flew over to Spence Bay where he had left a cache of supplies. He spent a week there, and learned that the new commissioner and his entourage of several councillors and their wives were to pay their first visit to the settlements. Harold was keen to meet them all and show them what he had been doing; however, his summer's work was all over in Pelly Bay.

The day they were to arrive by float-plane, the winds changed, blowing all the loose ice into the harbour. This necessitated a complete change of schedule. They would have to avoid Spence Bay and land in the next settlement, Pelly Bay. Harold had done quite a few favours for the administrator and did not have any compunction in asking him a favour in return. Bringing his supply of plaster, he flew off to Pelly with the administrator and his wife.

"I was just finishing modelling the bust of Theresa Kernak. It was the largest sculpture I had ever done in the arctic. I did all the mould casting entirely by myself, a very

Theresa Kernak,
Pelly Bay, NWT, 1968

heavy and formidable job. Now, with it and the seven other pieces, I would be able to inaugurate 'The World's First Art Exhibition in the Arctic'."

The VIPs were to arrive at 10:00 AM and the whole settlement was down at the rocky point to meet them. At that time the settlement consisted of one road and a half, totalling some 150 yards with nothing more for the visitors to see than a few dozen little houses and hundreds of miles of rocks and sea. Harold knew that the commissioner would be meeting the Inuit leaders and the missionaries for an hour or so, and there would be precious little for the women to do after walking the length of the settlement. The first member of the party to appear was Jake Oates, whom Harold knew quite well. Through him, he sent an invitation to the ladies to drop around to his house for tea after they had seen the settlement, and also to the men to come after their meeting.

"Feeling sure that my invitations would be accepted, I hastily ran down to Theresa's house and arranged for her to come up for a final sitting. None of the ladies had ever seen a sculptor at work and they were really pleased. Theresa was in good form and enjoyed the occasion. I prepared tea and biscuits. Drinks were forbidden at that time.

Not long after, the men all came in. Commissioner Hodgson was very impressed by the accurate likeness in my work. He had just acquired a Polaroid camera and used it profusely, amazing all as they watched the image develop; quite unbelievable!"

Hodgson took Harold aside and told him they were soon to build a new museum in Yellowknife and they must discuss the possibility of doing portraits of Inuit and Indians for the museum. In the following year, he hoped there would be a sum set aside in the budget for this purpose. The museum was eventually built and called the Prince of Wales Northern Heritage Centre. For many summers after that, Harold went up to the high arctic, sculpting for the museum and for the Glenbow in Calgary.

Mr. Hodgson was quite taken with Harold's dream of completing portraits of individuals representing all the circumpolar peoples. The commissioner's express wish was to have a collection of bronzes of Inuit from right around the world; the Polar Sea People. Harold had already sculpted some Alaskan Inuit and he said that he would try to get him to Greenland and maybe to Siberia one day to complete a unique collection of Inuit and Yuits.

Kenojuak is one of Canada's finest Inuit artists. She was born in 1927 in Cape Dorset, Baffin Island and baptised Kenojuak Ashavak. Collectors and museums are today paying phenomenal prices for her early prints. Harold's first acquaintance with Kenojuak was when she was a tubercular patient at the Hôpital du Parc Savard in Quebec City in 1954. In one of the wards there was an alcove large enough for two beds and the nurses had placed two friends in there. They were Tye of Lake Harbour and Kenojuak from Cape Dorset. Kenojuak and Tye were among those who showed great interest in the progress of Harold's portrait of Illya, the young boy who was his first Inuit subject. Both were exceptionally good at needlework and Harold kept them well supplied with material and beads to trim the rag dolls which they made for sale. There was always a waiting list for these dolls in the hospital shop. The miniature parkas and attigis which they made were real works of art, designed identically to those made for adults.

Many of the patients were declared cured some time before the ship was ready to return them to the north. The wait was difficult for them. On Sundays, Harold's doctor brother, Walter, took some of them for rides in his car to the zoo and on to the family home for supper.

"It was at our home that Kenojuak was first exposed to art: painting, sculpture, etchings and prints. My brother, whose hobby was painting, and who spoke some Inuktitut, was able to explain various techniques to her. She was pleased with some of his paintings which he had done in the north. I am sure that this early introduction to the world of art had a profound influence on her work. Indeed, in Jean Blodgett's impressive book on Kenojuak, she mentions both of us helping her in her art."

Kenojuak was among the patients returning to their homes on the ice breaker *C.D. Howe* in 1955, when Harold modelled her friend Tye.

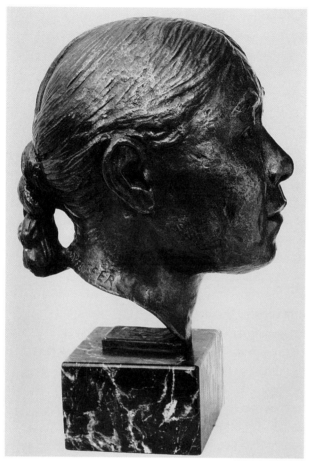

"It was about fifteen years later that Kenojuak posed for me when she came to Ottawa to be presented with the Order of Canada for her achievements in art. In the intervening years she had made a name for herself as the most important print-maker in the Arctic. She also ventured into stone carving with much success. Two of her designs, both of owls, have been chosen for Canadian stamps.

"The bronze portrait of Kenojuak illustrated here was accepted by the Royal Academy and exhibited in London in 1971. Since then, Kenojuak has been elected to membership in the Royal Canadian Academy of Art. In 1982 she was given the country's highest honour as a Companion of the Order of Canada. Her work can be seen in many of the world's finest museums and art galleries."

Although he was now quite busy arranging his life so that he could go to the arctic to pursue his commissions from both Riveredge and the Prince of Wales Northern Heritage Centre, Harold's habitual unabashed people-collecting still led him to do many portraits on his own initiative.

"I had just been to an exhibition of Inuit prints at a gallery in Ottawa and, in conversation with the owner, learned that my old friend Kenojuak was in town. As I was walking home, I noticed two parka-clad Inuit girls window-shopping. By their attire it was obvious that they had just come down from the North and by the shuffling of their feet, I knew that they were unused to walking on pavement. Approaching them, I was almost certain that the shorter one was Kenojuak, and I said "Hello Kenojuak." She turned around suddenly and said she was not Kenojuak, but said that she knew her. Embarrassed, I apologized for my mistake, and we got into conversation. Having lived in and visited so many arctic settlements over the years, I rarely have trouble identifying people I have met.

"The girl whom I had mistaken for my friend spoke English, but it was her companion, Elizapee from Sugluk, who attracted me. They were both guests of a nurse who had worked in the north and now lived in Ottawa. I had a definite interest in Sugluk for I had been there many years previously and more recently had done the head of one of my godsons, Adamie Kalingo, who also came from there. It turned out that Adamie was a cousin of hers. I had also known the Anglican missionary, the Rev. Mr. Ellis, who had been there for some years.

"Elizapee had a most unusual moon-face, with very full, almost negroid lips and very pronounced almond-shaped eyes. I had a great desire to sculpt her. It was early in the evening and this was too good an opportunity to miss. I followed up at once and asked them to come to my studio. It was not a "come up and see me sometime" approach but come NOW. So they agreed and I drew them a diagram of how to find my house. I was two streets down and one over to the left and I expected them at 7:30.

"I waited until 8:00 and finally went out on the street and walked down to the corner where they stood together giggling. They had passed by my house several times but were shy about coming in. However, they returned with me.

"After showing them my collection of early Inuit carvings and the bronzes I had done, I asked Elizapee if she would pose for me. An empathy was growing between us and she agreed. I immediately got my calipers and took the basic measurements of her head so that I could build up the rough clay before she came back for a proper sitting the next evening. They didn't have any engagements so I suggested that they come over after 7:00 the next evening. They both agreed. It happened that their hostess was taking courses at the university every evening until 10:00 PM. I gave them tea and cookies; I took them to the corner, with full instructions for how to get home and off they went.

"Next evening, I waited in vain. I phoned their house but got no answer. The following day I phoned again and finally contacted the nurse, and she gave me a thorough scolding! This was the girls' first time in a city, in fact the first time they had been to any place with a population of over 200 souls! The nurse had told them not to wander off Elgin Street and she had returned to find no one home. The only person whom the girls could have visited was Kenojuak, so she went over there and found no one in. As is the custom in the Arctic, if there is a light on in a house, tent or igloo and one wishes to visit, one goes in at any hour without any inhibitions.

"Apparently, upon leaving my house, the girls called on Kenojuak, had found it too hot and decided to go for a walk and returned about 12:30 AM. The nurse was nearly frantic and all the more so when the girls announced that they had met a man and had gone to his house! Well! They did not remember his name but said that he had lived in the arctic and had made many "pictures" of Inuit out of "mud." When she calmed down and saw my card, she was somewhat

Chief Dan George
OC, 1969

mollified. Sittings were resumed the next day.

"I always remunerate my native sitters for their time. However, this had not come up in my conversation with them. When I completed the bust, it was an unexpected surprise when I gave them each some money for their cooperation. Now they could go shopping for real.

"In 1970 I had an invitation to exhibit at the National Portrait Gallery in London, England and was very pleased when the jury selected Padlayat's bust for exhibition. This was a great honour. I was told that this was the first time a Canadian artist had been accepted at the gallery. Friends who visited the gallery said that there were always a few people standing around it, curious and interested."

Harold's portrait of Dan George is also a product of a chance encounter. It is said that when Dan George was first at school, his teachers could not pronounce his Indian name, Tes-Wah-No, and they called him Dan George. He was a Coast Salish Indian. When he was quite young, he started work as a logger, then for twenty-eight years he was a longshoreman, mostly around the Burrard Peninsula near where he was born in 1899. His son Robert was active in play groups and the Little Theatre, and when they needed someone who could play the part of an old Indian, Robert suggested his father and the rest is history. Dan took to it naturally, and from then on, his career was in acting, on stage and TV, until Hollywood discovered him. He performed in *Little Big Man*, with Dustin Hoffman, with such distinction that he was nominated for an Academy Award. He also appeared in *A Different Drummer* and *The Youngest Warrior*.

He was not only a fine actor but a wise philosopher. His poetry and prose are both deep and moving. He published two books, *My Heart Soars* and *My Spirit Soars*, and he was a guest on Roy Bonisteel's program *Man Alive*, sharing his philosophy of life. In 1972 he was Parade Marshall at the Calgary Stampede. The country's highest honour was bestowed on him when the Governor-General presented him with the Order of Canada.

"I first met Dan in 1969. I had just returned from a three-month trip sculpting Inuit in the arctic. After a performance of the National Ballet at the National Arts Centre, my friends drove to their country house and I walked home. I am in the habit of having a snack before I retire and, passing the Lord Elgin Hotel, decided to go in and have something to eat.

"Most of the tables were occupied with theatre-goers. Sitting alone at a table was this very distinguished Indian with long grey hair, wearing a buckskin jacket. Immediately attracted to him, I asked if I might join him. Over the years I had had much to do with Indians of many nations and we got into a pleasant conversation. He informed me that he was acting in a play at the National Arts Centre called *The Ecstasy of Rita Joe* and was to be in the city for a full week. He had a very magnetic presence, his face timeworn and tranquil. I asked if he could spare the time to pose for me and he said that he was free every day from 5:00 until 7:00 PM. He agreed to come to my studio at 5:15 every day and pose before leaving for rehearsals. After the sitting I would take him to a nearby restaurant for supper. This time was an extra dividend for me for I could continue to study his facial features while we ate. In a week I had the portrait finished and I had six casts made of it.

"For several years, on my annual visits to Vancouver, I visited him. I found him a delightful gentleman and was proud to be one of his friends. Dan passed away in 1981 and the funeral was held in Holy Rosary Cathedral in Vancouver. Over 1,200 mourners were in attendance."

The Glenbow Museum quickly expanded the scope of their commissions for Harold to include notable western Indian chiefs. Jimmie Bruneau was a highly respected chief of the Dogrib tribe. At one time he had been a heavy drinker, smoker and gambler but he gave it all up and tried to influence the younger people of the tribe to do the same. He was ninety-four years old and very frail at the time Harold did his portrait; nevertheless, he lived to see it cast in bronze and ensconced in the lobby of a fine new school named after him in Edzo, some nine miles west of Fort Rae. When the Jimmie Bruneau School was officially opened by Jean Chretien, then Minister of Northern Affairs, Chief Bruneau unveiled his own bust. He said it was the greatest day of his life.

He passed away soon afterwards and the whole community turned out to honour him in the biggest funeral ever to have taken place in Fort Rae. After resting in the lobby of the Jimmy Bruneau School for more than twenty years, the bust was stolen. It has since been replaced with a second cast in bronze.

"Getting his permission to do his head was the hardest part of the assignment. I had been warned before going to Fort Rae that he might not approve of the project and that if he once said "no," his word would be final. Consequently I didn't want to make a direct approach but had to work out a careful strategy.

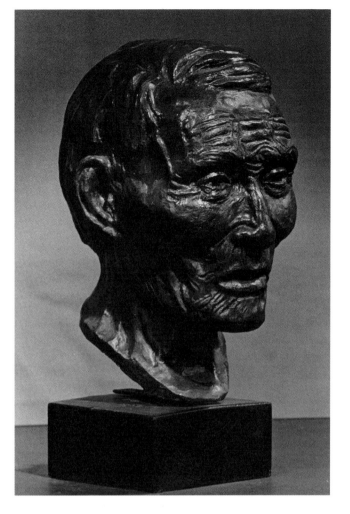

Chief Jimmy Bruneau,
Fort Rae, NWT, 1971

"I also had a commission to sculpt a sub-chief, Alexis Charlo, who was an intimate friend of Jimmy Bruneau's. We agreed that the best strategy for getting the old chief's interest was to start on Alexis, and, as word spread about the portrait, Bruneau would come and take a look.

"I got to know Alexis' eldest son, Charlie, quite well and I asked him if he thought his father would sit for me. At the time Charlie was a councillor in the settlement and spoke good English and frequently acted as an interpreter. He willingly took me to his father's house one evening and explained my proposition to him.

"When Alexis heard that the Commissioner of the Northwest Territories was anxious to have it done for the new museum in Yellowknife and that it was to be cast in bronze, he was very pleased and gave his approval.

"All this was complicated by the fact that I had arrived in Fort Rae just a week before Easter. This was by design, for I knew Easter was one of the great celebrations of the Dogribs and I wanted to be there for it. What I didn't know was just what an important occasion it was and just how early it started. By the time I arrived, friends and relatives from a one-hundred-mile radius had descended upon the community. Every house was bursting with people and bustling with activity. There was much drinking and gambling and a general party atmosphere pervaded the settlement. No one was interested in serious appointments.

"Alexis was one of the most prosperous men in the community. For this reason it did not occur to me that I should offer to pay him for posing for me as I usually did for most of my native sitters. This proved to be a mistake. I made at least four trips to his house to take the measurements of his head and face and each time left without them. Twice his wife indicated that Alexis had a headache and was lying down. On the other occasions I found him squatting on the floor with four or five other men playing cards and gambling. There was no question of interrupting him.

"Obviously there was a problem, and someone in the community suggested that money was probably at the back of his excuses. The answer to the problem was simple. We went to his house with his son to rectify the matter. While the arrangements for sittings and appropriate payments were soon made, I ran into other difficulties. His house was built on a hill of sloping rock which was usually ice-covered from the waste-water thrown out the kitchen door. Because of the rocks there was a long walk to the front door. This made carrying the clay bust up to the house quite hazardous and it had to be carried away again when I left. This was not a household in which to leave a precious piece of art unattended; there was a steady stream of lively grandchildren and others coming and going at all times of the day and night.

"After the first sitting at his house, we arranged that future sittings would take place where I was staying, at the home of Peter Anderson, the settlement administrator, about thirty yards below Alexis' place. I caught his likeness quickly and the word soon spread around about the fellow who was making a head out of mud. For the rest of our sittings I had a large audience of curious youngsters and some adults as well. But no Chief Jimmy Bruneau.

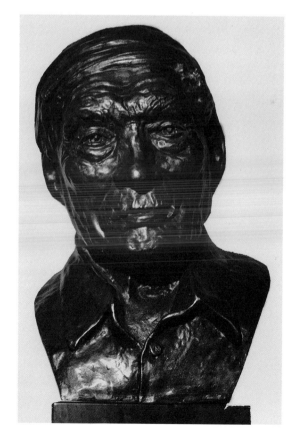

Alexis Charlo,
Fort Rae, NWT, 1971

"Alexis had a fine strong face with very prominent cheekbones and wonderful deep lines of joy and sorrow etched on his forehead and radiating around his eyes. Although he was respected for his great and wise counsel in the community, he was not a Dogrib; he was a Chipewyan. He passed away in 1993.

"It was Dr. George Gibson, with whom I was staying at the time, who finally introduced me to the old man. Chief Bruneau had an appointment with him at the hospital. Dr. Gibson suggested that when the examination was over, the sisters would bring him into the dining lounge for a cup of tea and that I should be there with my albums of photographs and my calipers. One of the priests agreed to interpret for me. First I wanted to take measurements of his face with my calipers and take some photographs of him and have them enlarged. Because of his age, and the fact that he had a bad heart, I felt it would be wise, just in case he passed away before I was finished.

"I was somewhat apprehensive about this because, although most of the natives were devout church-going Roman Catholics, as was the Chief, some of the old people were still superstitious about having photographs taken of themselves. There was active resentment among the older natives of the intrusion of white culture, and I feared the Chief might refuse me on that account.

"It all went according to plan. When he came in for tea, I showed him photographs of other chiefs I had sculpted and the Father explained what the calipers were for. However, I still had a problem. When the Chief gave up drinking and smoking, he had substituted chewing gum. This he did with great gusto using his three remaining teeth. His jaw was working in every direction, which made it impossible to get accurate measurements. I tried imitating his jaw action and then to show him I wanted him to stop chewing, I put my hand up to his chin to keep his jaw closed. He thought I wanted his gum, and spat it out into my hand. The sisters who were also having a tea break and watching the whole procedure burst out laughing. The old Chief also saw the fun of it and finally relaxed.

"After it was all over and we were driving him home, we discovered that the Chief apparently thought that when I took his measurements, it was part of the medical treatment. He said that no doctor had ever done this to him before. I was getting nowhere!

"A few days later, the doctor had to visit him again. This time he suggested that I go along as his assistant and hold the stethoscope. This was the opportunity I was looking for. We sat him in front of the window with the sun shining in on him and we listened to his heart. Then I took a series of photographs and the doctor gave him some pills. I think he still thought my doings were part of the medical procedure. His wife was blind, and also had no idea what I wanted. I still didn't know whether or not he was going to let me do his portrait, or pose properly for me.

"It wasn't until the evening of the big Easter feast that I got my answer. We all assembled at the Community Hall following a volley of shots which announced the beginning of the celebrations. Everyone arrived carrying a large bowl, a spoon, a mug and a hand towel or wash cloth. There were chairs for the chiefs and the rest of us squatted on the floor in long lines, face to face, men on one side of the room and women on the other, all about eighteen

83

Willie Scraping White, Blood Reserve, Cardston, Alberta, 1972

inches apart. Oilcloth was unrolled between us and this served as a tablecloth and a runway for the men serving us so we had to guard our shins as well as our bowls as the waiters passed by. One by one the men served, first a ladle of hot oatmeal, then a spoonful of jam, a ration of canned peaches, hard boiled eggs, caribou ribs and finally hot tea biscuits and bread. No one touched their food. The next man to pass by carried an empty wash basin in which every guest deposited either cigarettes, pipe tobacco or matches. These were offerings to the gods, to be burned in a traditional ceremony outside. Another hour and a half was taken up with speeches welcoming the neighbouring chiefs and with their replies, most of which were in a local dialect and had to be translated into Dogrib. Finally, the god of the white man was appeased with a traditional blessing and the feast began.

"Through all of this, I was seated conspicuously, cross-legged on the floor, at the feet of Chief Bruneau, the first in the row. This turned out to be fortunate for me. The priest who was seated on a chair beside the old Chief pointed to me and said, "That's the fellow who is going to do your head in clay." The old man replied, "When is he going to start?"

"After that, things were easily arranged. Every day we sent the hospital station wagon over for him and he posed for me at the doctor's house. He was very cooperative and always spat out his gum before entering the house. Because of his age, we made the sittings short. I always made him tea and gave him biscuits to dunk. He would walk around the house, look at the pictures in the magazines and seemed to enjoy the sittings and the general change of scene.

"When the bust was finished, I had a little party at the house to thank those who had helped me, including the doctor, the two Fathers, the Sisters from the hospital and, of course, my honoured sitter, the Chief. He was very animated and very pleased about the bust."

"Even at ninety-four, Willie Scraping White was an impressive looking man. I was having a cup of tea in Cardston's only restaurant the first time I saw him. A big man, he walked slowly by the window supporting himself on a cane. He had a naturally ruddy complexion which, I found out later, he aided cosmetically by the addition of copper lustre. That day he was wearing a battered old ten-gallon stetson hat and two skimpy black braids tied in red ribbons straggled down his back. Later, when I saw him without his hat, I found that his hair in the front was snow white, combed into a pompadour and powdered with sacred red earth. A bright kerchief around his neck added to his colourful appearance.

"Naturally I was intrigued, especially as he had good bone structure and a high brow, a long face and protuberant lower lip, all of which added up to an interesting subject for sculpture. When I enquired about him, I found that he was a well known and highly respected medicine man of the Blood tribe. He was known as "Napi" by the Indians and was recognized by band members as a spiritual advisor and leading authority on Indian religious rites. The word "napi" is used in a number of ways in the Blackfoot language, depending on pronunciation. It can mean "friend" or be a greeting for an old man, or it can refer to The Old Man of legend, a prankster and troublemaker. The sun is sometimes named "Napi," or "old man."

"He was also reputed to be a devout Anglican and had been the second pupil to enrol at the St. Paul's Anglican Residential School on the reserve when it opened in 1890. Napi was a member of the Horn Society and religious rites were very much part of his daily life as I discovered the first time I visited him to ask him to pose for me.

"I had arranged with a cowboy named Morris Curlis to drive me the nine miles from Cardston to the small one-room house where he lived on the reserve with his younger brother, Yellow Bull, who was eighty-seven. Next door, his granddaughter and her family lived in a slightly larger house. As we approached the two houses at the end of a long dirt road, Morris gave me some sound advice which I have followed ever since. "A stranger must never drive right up to the door," he said, "go slowly, park the car a distance away, and then walk toward the house."

"This, he explained, gives the occupants time to draw back a corner of the curtain and peek out. The visitor is hurriedly discussed, and then the woman of the house is warned and she might do a quick tidy-up job. If she thinks the visitor is acceptable, he will then be permitted to come into the house; if not, he is left standing on the stoop. In this case we were also announced by three barking dogs and three small children who appeared immediately. They willingly carried our message to their great-grandfather and came back to say that Napi would see me.

"The two brothers had been resting and were still on their beds. The room was neat and tidy, especially considering that everything they needed for daily living was there in the one room. It contained two double beds with a dresser beside each, a small table, a box on which there was a jug and basin for washing up and a small sideboard.

"Above each of their beds hung drums and pipe bundles partly covered with cloths and I later learned that they were used in sacred ceremonies for the Horn Society. On the floor between the two beds were two bowls. Yellow Bull greeted me and Napi beckoned me to come and sit beside him on his bed. I almost made a very grave error by attempting to step over, instead of going around, the two bowls. They were sacred vessels for the sweat-bath ceremony.

"To explain to him what I wanted was not easy. As I talked I produced my album of other Indians I had sculpted in bronze to show him. These were obviously very strange to him and he said jokingly, "You want to kill me and cut off my head?"

Chief Jim Shot Both Sides,
Blood Reserve, Cardston,
Alberta, 1972

"I tried to explain the procedure to him. I told him how it started with a likeness made in clay which was then made into a plaster cast and finally into a bronze head. His reaction to this was, 'Clay, clay, I don't want my head dirtied in mud.' To reassure him that I would not dirty him, I showed him a photograph of me working on the portrait of an Inuit woman. Clean and untouched, she stood beside me and her portrait.

"Finally we got down to basics. I told him that all he had to do was sit still for a short time each day for a few days and for this I would pay him. Then he agreed to pose for me. We arranged that I should come every morning for the next few days. The old man tired easily and had to have frequent breaks. He had a very pronounced lower lip of which he was very conscious and while he did, in general, approve of my work, he felt I was exaggerating this physical characteristic. At his insistence I did reduce it a fraction but he still was not satisfied.

"Several times his religious duties conflicted with our sittings. His friends came to bring him to a sweat lodge. This is like a sauna, and is a spiritual ceremony; not only is the body cleansed but the soul is refreshed by prayer. Napi's presence was always in demand by the elders at these ceremonies because he was known for his eloquent and meaningful prayers. I was told, though, that the children found his prayers frightfully long, especially as they were always delivered in the Blood language which not all the young people understood.

"One day when Napi was posing for me, a starling flew into the house. In its futile attempts to escape, the terrified bird crashed repeatedly into the glass window panes. I tried to catch it but the bird had practically knocked itself senseless by the time I finally managed it. As often was the case, the three great-grandchildren were watching me and became very excited as I finally caught the bird. I gently straightened out its feathers and carried it out to the porch, hoping it might revive and fly away. The children were astonished, and I later learned that in their belief, it is a very bad omen to have a bird fly into the house or teepee and it should be killed at once.

"Strangely enough, when the bust was completed and cast in bronze, the first time it was shown, someone commented on the fact that Napi had a bird alighting on his chest. The "bird" was formed by the curl of a ribbon which tied up one of his braids and could only be seen at certain angles. I was astonished when I saw it that way, but it was probably meant to be.

"Willie Scraping White died on September 18th, 1974. He had been born in Red Crow's cabin, the first log structure built near Standoff, Alberta in 1877. He outlived five wives and had been the spiritual advisor to four generations of Blood Indians. For seventy-five years he had been a practising Medicine Man. As a "healer through prayers," or "Holy Man," as he was known, he had a tremendous influence on his community. It was said that he named thousands of young Blood children during his career and that he generally bestowed an appropriate name on them by being able to predict their future personality. His bronze bust is in the Glenbow Museum in Calgary. Later, I sculpted a half-size bust of him, and it was a very popular item."

Jim Shot Both Sides is descended from a long line of well known Indians. His great-grandfather Red Crow was a famous Chief of the Band at the signing of Treaty No. 7, in September 1877, a treaty which bound the protection of the Indians under Queen Victoria. They had rations, treaty money, clothing, blankets, ammunition, etc., and were to live in peaceful coexistence with the people of Canada.

Following in the footsteps of a renowned grandfather and father must be an awesome challenge. Jim's father was hereditary head Chief of the Bloods for forty-three years. The old chief was highly regarded for his wisdom and businesslike qualities and his chieftainship was rarely challenged. He is remembered for his encouragement of the old ways and for his defense of his people's rights. After his death in 1956, in long-accepted tribal fashion, his son Jim was chosen to succeed him. It is said that as he was so well known and revered that he never campaigned during election time and at the elections in 1972, he was returned to the chieftainship by sixty-four percent of the votes.

"October 26, 1973 saw the opening of the Shot Both Sides Complex in Standoff, Alberta. This was named for his late father but can also be said to be a thank-you to his son, the present chief of the tribe. This fine complex of buildings contains the administration offices of the Blood Tribe, a bank, a pharmacy, an outpatients clinic, public health offices, dental offices, a post office, a shopping centre and an Indian Affairs office. The completion of the planning, building and financing of this enterprise was in no small measure due to Jim's great interest in it. Another important event during Jim's chieftainship was the opening of the Kainai Industries Limited plant, a sectional housing manufacturing operation, also in Standoff. Jim had much to do with the organization and planning of this enterprise when it first opened.

"He was educated at St. Mary's R.C. Residential School on the reserve. In 1956, when the electoral system was introduced, he was defeated but was re-elected in 1968 and at each successive election, he has retained the chieftainship. He is a good leader and has kept up with modern thought. He has a farm, is married and has fourteen children. His bust is now in the Glenbow Museum in Calgary".

Mrs. Janie Gladstone was born in Cardston, Alberta in 1895, the daughter of Joe Healey, who was an Indian scout and interpreter on the Blood Reserve. He is remembered as a well-known and highly respected man. Mrs. Gladstone attended the Anglican Mission

Janie Gladstone, Cardston, Alberta, 1972

boarding school, St. Paul's Residential School, on the reserve, and was active in the Women's Auxilliary of St. Paul's Church.

She was the mother of four daughters and two sons who contribute greatly to the well-being of their people. They are active in the Indian news media, outstanding in educational and business affairs and in industry. Her sons and grandsons are also very active in rodeos and other sporting events.

"As the wife of Senator James Gladstone, Canada's first native senator, Mrs. Gladstone came to Ottawa to be with her husband when the Senate was sitting. A rather shy person, she did not especially enjoy the many functions which a senator's spouse is more or less obliged to attend. However, she enjoyed going to functions at Government House, because Madame Vanier, who was the Chatelaine at the time, always had an affectionate hug and kiss for Mrs. Gladstone and made her feel most welcome.

"Cardston, being a small town, has no night life. It is a Mormon town, and I was not made welcome in people's homes as I had become accustomed to elsewhere. I stayed in a tiny motel room with no radio, television and no books. However, I was very pleased to spend many evenings enjoying the warm hospitality of the Gladstone home. She was an excellent sitter and I think that the special empathy between us helped me greatly in creating what I think is a good likeness of her. The bronze is in the Glenbow Museum in Calgary."

"I was visiting my friend the late Dr. George Gooderham in Calgary when he showed me some photographs of some Indians in nearby Cluny and Gleichen. Seeing the photo of One Gun, I was immediately captivated by his wonderful face and proud looks. He was a man I had to meet.

"Over the years, press reports about One Gun's age varied. When he died in the Bassano Hospital on December 15, 1973, an excellent obituary appeared in the Kainai News, written by a relative. She stated that he was born in Spitzee (High River) about 1874, which made him a centenarian. I don't know if the date is accurate, but he looked that age. One writer said that in the early days, the Blackfoot called him "Wolf Collar" because his robe was made of wolf skins. However, all the old Indians of the tribe called him "One Gun" which was the name his father before him was called. (In Canada the tribe is called Blackfoot whereas in the United States, they are known as the Blackfeet.)

"He was a recognized authority on Indian culture and, for many years, ethnologists from far and wide, with the aid of interpreters, consulted him for information on many tribal customs, various secret societies, the meaning of many things beyond the ken of contemporary younger natives. He didn't speak any English; he only spoke a very old form of Blackfoot, which often taxed the interpreters.

"He was a gentle old man with outstanding features, a thin face, broken nose, heavily wrinkled brow, cheeks and lips very furrowed. Just about every-thing about him fascinated me, though I knew that here was a real challenge for me to record his likeness well. Fortunately an empathy developed immedi-ately between us and work progressed. Sitting on a hard chair was tiring for him, so every ten or fifteen minutes I suggested that he get up and walk around to take the kinks out.

"For many years, One Gun sat on the Council and was also a minor chief for a period. As a young man he worked as a miner in his own drift coal mines on the south bank of the Bow River. He is said to have had an uncanny gift for knowing where many of the drifts were located. After that he had a small farm, but was an indifferent farmer.

"He was always known and respected as a devout man and was over the years a member of the Prairie Chickens, Brave Dogs and the Horn Societies. During his life he had married three times; his wives all predeceased him. He was a good sitter and I felt that I captured a good likeness of him. This was done in the spring of 1972 and is in the Glenbow Museum.

"When "The Greatest Outdoor Show on Earth" (the Stampede) started in 1911, One Gun was there with his white stallion and a wagon team. His hailstone tipi was always erected in the Indian Village of the Stampede. The hailstone design came to his ancestor, One Chief, from a spirit in the clouds. He will be remembered for a long while; he left a heritage of knowledge of Indian culture for all time.

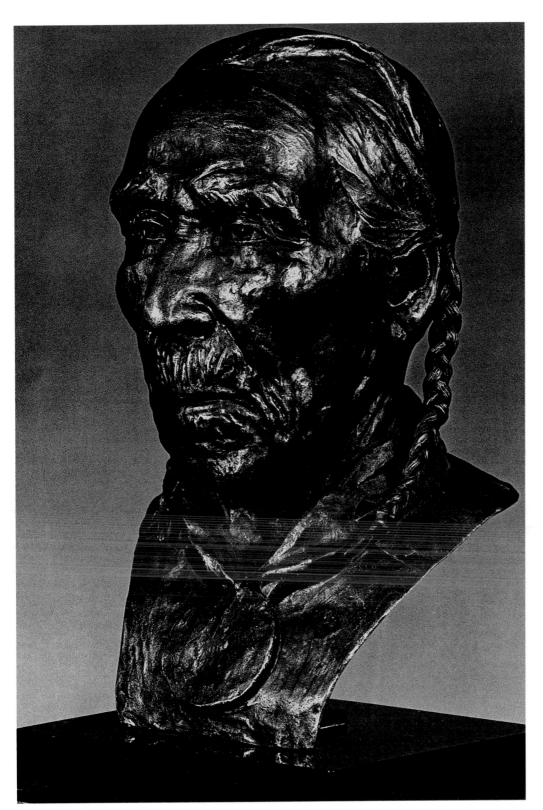

One Gun, Blackfoot, Cluny,
Alberta, 1972

91

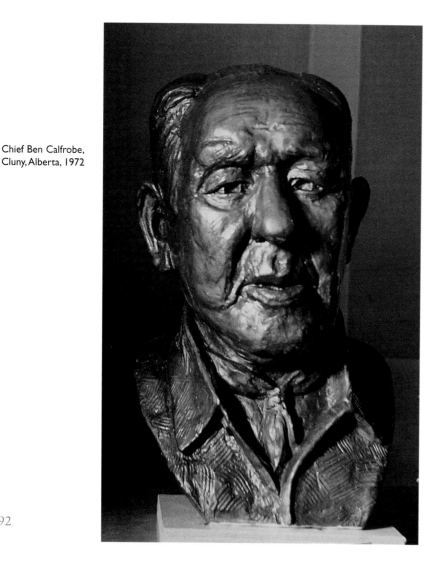

Chief Ben Calfrobe,
Cluny, Alberta, 1972

"Chief Ben Calfrobe posed for me at his home in Cluny, Alberta in 1972. He was born in a tipi on the Blackfoot reserve in 1890, the youngest son of a signer of Treaty Number 7. In 1908 he became a scout for the Royal Northwest Mounted Police on the reserve and remained in that position for nineteen years. He studied farming at the Calgary industrial school and decided to set himself up in that line.

"He was a great supporter of the Calgary Stampede and attended yearly until his death in 1979. After he was named a minor chief for life in 1930, he set up his tipi every year at the Indian Village at the Stampede. The motif on his tipi was the buffalo. He was a member of the Beaver Society, the Horn Society and the Sun Dance Society. For some years he was active in politics and, whenever he could, he attended important pow-wows.

"The last time I spoke to him was at a big pow-wow in Ottawa in 1977 and he told me how the Prairie Chicken Society started: "An old man came from the Sand Hills and it was getting dark, so he slept there. During his sleep, he dreamed of chickens dancing. Towards morning he heard a strange noise like tapping, like a rattle in the wind. Then in his dream he saw a big circle of prairie chickens around him and every time they passed him they flapped their wings. This same scene came to him many times after. When he came home, he taught this dance to his sons; he painted their faces with yellow spots on one side of the face and body and green spots on the other side." The Prairie Chicken Society became an important means of educating the young in the traditions of the Blackfoot.

"Ben had a very full life, and gave much in return to his people. In his book *Siksika: A Blackfoot Legacy*, he tells the story of his education in white man's schools, and shares his great knowledge of tribal societies, the wisdom and culture of his people. He also arranged for films to be made of the Sun Dance and other ceremonies, which many felt were too sacred to be shared with the uninitiated. If he had not done this, much might have been lost forever. The bronze of Ben Calfrobe is in the Glenbow Museum".

"Although ninety-five years old at the time he sat for this portrait, Chief Julien Yendo still rose every morning at 6:00 AM to have a paddle before breakfast. This involved climbing down the steep road to the Mackenzie River from the high bank on which Fort Wrigley stood, and launching his canoe.

"He was a very jovial sitter and the warmth between him and his eighty-five-year-old wife and their grandchildren, who often accompanied them, was unmistakable, even though I could not understand the Slavey language in which they talked. All the same, he did not forget that he was a Chief and set up his own protocol in our dealings. This I came to understand only gradually.

"When I approached him about sitting for me, and explained my purpose and that I would pay him, the old Chief had a chat with his wife in Slavey and then nodded his approval. We set up an arrangement for the first sitting and I returned to where I was staying.

"My nephew Reg had flown me up in his plane and we had arranged to rent a house on the main street. There were only two streets in the settlement. A short distance away was the one and only store, The Bay. The Chief's log house was in a small stand of trees facing the gravel roadway of the other street.

"When Chief Yendo had not arrived by 2:00, the time we had set for the sitting the following day, I was not surprised, as I had discovered that native people attached little importance to time in relation to appointments. When it reached 3:00 PM and he still hadn't come, I decided to go over and investigate. When I knocked on the door, the chief appeared, grabbed his battered old hat, walked out in front of me and off we went.

"The sitting went well. Reg kept him well supplied with tea, biscuits and cigarettes. I walked him back home and it was arranged, through the children, that he arrive the next morning at 9:00 AM.

"The next morning it was the same story; he did not arrive at the designated hour. Time was precious to me, and I did not wait so long to go after him. As I came to the door, he grabbed his cap and again walked out in front of me. I concluded that he felt that, in his position as chief, he should demand this sign of respect from me, so every day, I went to call for him and walked him back home later, careful always to let him enter and exit in front of me.

"He established a daily routine as he came into our house. Reg usually met him at the door, saluted him, clicking his heels together in a very military manner and saying a warm "Hello Chief." The old man responded by throwing up his

Chief Julien Yendo, Fort
Wrigley, NWT, 1972

94

hands and giving a shout. Then he would do a little tap-dance on the door stoop. His wife usually came over with the grandchildren to watch the modelling process. Occasionally she would playfully give him a poke or push his head aside or rumple his hair. It amused Julien to goose his grandchildren as they passed by him. They followed the progress of my work very closely. As the work took on his traits, word spread and half the community must have come in to see the sculpture. There was complete silence until some elder made a comment in Slavey, and then there was much animated chatter that seemed to complete their acceptance and all the older men patted me on the shoulder, quite satisfied that I'd done a good job on their chief. I found that this procedure became almost routine in most settlements and it was very gratifying to me.

"In our more relaxed moments, when we had tea, I asked him to sing some old songs. His voice was pretty creaky and would have grated on some people, but it was music to my ears because I was so interested. I regret that I did not have my tape recorder with me. His bust in bronze is in the Prince of Wales Heritage Centre in Yellowknife."

"I first saw Johnny Powderface one evening while sitting in the grandstand watching the horse races in Calgary. I had just arrived in the west to start working on a commission from the Riveredge Foundation to do portrait sculptures of some of the Plains Indians of Alberta. My companion, Dr. Margaret (Marmee) Hess, a ranch owner and breeder of race horses, was totally engrossed in the activity of the track and gave me a running commentary on the parentage of each horse, the ranch it came from, any previous wins, the jockey on each one.

"It was all very interesting but...there were quite a few Indians below us in the crowd and although I certainly like horses, I must confess that my eyes and mind were focused on the former rather than the latter. To my delight, a most distinctive old Indian gentleman dressed in an old unmatched suit, with moccasins on his feet, walked up the steps and sat on an aisle seat just across from me. He had a whimsical face and many lines of joy and sorrow etched from the corners of his eyes and down his cheeks; a joy to a sculptor. His nose and cheekbones were pronounced. His keen eyes followed the scene intensely and he obviously was not a novice, for, between the races, he studiously followed the racing form with great interest. His appearance made me think that, in his youth, he might have been one of my boyhood heroes, an Indian scout. His face was framed by two wispy braids of grey hair, tied up with rawhide thong.

"I discussed him with Marmee and she agreed that he would make an excellent subject for a bronze bust. She said she thought she had seen him in the Morley district near her ranch and that he was probably of the Stoney tribe. Just as my inhibitions subsided and I was about to go and talk to him, he got up and left the grandstand.

Johnny Powderface, Morley, Alberta, 1972

96

"Fortunately for me, several months later, when I was in Morley sculpting Tom Kaquitts, I met him in the administration building on the reserve. I found that he spoke excellent English and, as a child, had gone to the McDougall Mission School in Morley. He was a great lover of horses and never missed a good race.

"I particularly liked his rather shy and quiet-spoken manner and he proved to be an excellent sitter. He was a councillor of the Chiniquay Band of the Stoneys for about fifteen years. His son Frank Powderface was also a councillor and later chief of the same band until December 1973, when the three bands amalgamated and a new chief was elected in the person of Frank Kaquitts. The following year, when I was in Morley, I sculpted Frank Kaquitts."

"While sculpting portrait heads of Indians in Cluny, Alberta I received a commission from the Riveredge Foundation to do two prominent Indians in nearby Gleichen. They were Chief Joe Crowfoot and Earl Calf Child. The communities were near each other and news had spread about me. In conversation, I heard that Joe might be a tough customer to handle, and probably difficult to find too; he might be at home, or maybe at his daughter's or at the tavern.

"I phoned his home one Friday and found him there. He was very pleased to have his head done for a museum. We planned the first sitting for the following Monday, at his home, and I wrote down the directions for getting there. They sounded quite involved, so I said that I would take a taxi.

"I called on Sister Celine again. She was a great person and one of the few who had a car. She taxied many of the Indians to and from the hospital and for

special events. Before leaving on Monday, knowing his reputation, she phoned Crowfoot first. Sure enough, he was, "not here, he's in hospital." We found him at the hospital, his face black and blue, with stitches in his cheek. He had been in a family "squabble" Saturday night and had to be taken to the hospital. The nurse said that he could go home and asked if we would take him in our taxi. He was in a good mood and told us that he had "beaten the shit" out of a fellow Saturday night, and indeed, when we went into his house, sure enough, there was his victim, flaked out on a bed in the living room with a few scars on his back. At this time, Joe Crowfoot was seventy-eight years old.

Chief Joe Crowfoot, Gleichen, Alberta, 1972

97

"Joe let me take measurements of his head with the calipers which I had brought with me and I took a few photographs of him as well. As to finding his home, I realized that the directions he had given me were altogether too vague and felt it wiser for our future sittings to

Tom Kaquitts,
Morley, Alberta, 1972

98

have him come over to the Old Sun College, where I was staying. I said that I would pay for the taxi trips.

"Joe's grandfather was a warrior and a great chief. As head of the Blackfoot, he signed Treaty No. 7 in 1877, and forbade his tribe to engage in the Northwest Rebellion in 1885. In Joe's youth he was a keen sportsman, taking part in every rodeo available. Travelling through Alberta in summer, one can hardly find a village or town that does not have a grandstand with rodeos scheduled regularly until fall. The pros turn up whenever the prizes are worth their while. Joe said he never missed a good rodeo.

"One year he helped organize a team of young fellows to go to Australia for calf roping and other rodeo events. Going on a large ocean liner was a special thrill for him. He told me one day that when he had been asked up to the "captain's house" the captain let him "run the boat" for an hour or so." Was easy, it warn't hard at all. There weren't no traffic," said he. He was quite a talker. He kept me entertained while I sculpted him. He passed away on December 17, 1976 in his eighty-second year. At his funeral, Leo Pretty Young Man, chief of the Blackfoot tribe, said, "Joe played a major role in leading his people in all fields of endeavour." The bronze I made of him is in the Glenbow Museum."

Chief Sitting Wind,
Frank Kaquitts, Morely,
Alberta, 1972

99

Helen Kalvak CC, RCA, Holman Island, NWT, 1974

Arctic Portraits, 1974-1979

Helen Kalvak's sitting was a challenge for Harold. She was an important and very successful Inuit artist, and her bust was commissioned by the Prince of Wales Northern Heritage Centre. He arrived in the settlement so severely chilled by a plane ride next to a broken window that he could not get off the seaplane without help. She sat for him in her combined living room, dining room and kitchen. With some difficulty, he persuaded her to sit in a straight-backed chair.

Kalvak's grandson, an extremely active and spoiled boy of three, resented the sculptor's presence. "He had a large screwdriver and frequently plunged it into the large glob of plasticine I was using. Once, I grabbed it away from him and he set up an awful howl and I had to give it back. Then he started to poke me with it. Customarily Inuit children are not reprimanded and I soon learned to mind my own business."

Luckily some visitors came in and the child calmed down. One day, he wanted something on the top shelf of the cabinet laden with cans and bottles. He climbed on a chair and the whole top section of the cabinet collapsed onto him. He emerged spattered with jam and molasses. Session over.

Kalvak's commercial success was much helped by the interest which Father Henri Tardif showed in her work. Tardif was an Oblate priest from Vivier, France. Kalvak enjoyed drawing scenes showing traditional activities such as fishing and hunting, household chores, tending the wicks on the kudliks, cutting up game, and drying and smoking fish for winter storage. Many of her designs were printed on cloth and sold as wall-hangings, pictures, calendars and greeting cards. Encouraging Kalvak and other talented people in the settlement, Father Tardif started an art co-op which soon became a profitable enterprise and an outlet to commerce in the South. For her important contribution to Art, Kalvak was made a member of the Royal Canadian Academy of Arts and some years later she received Canada's highest honour, Companion of the Order of Canada. Kalvak died in 1984, aged eighty-three.

"I sculpted Kalvak on the Island in 1974. She is said to have descended from a long line of shamans and as a young woman, practised this form of healing sorcery. When I sculpted her she was not very well and I heard that she enjoyed ill health in that she particularly looked forward to the daily visits of the nurse, who administered pink pills to her.

"She had a slightly square face with a double line of tattoos in a "Y" formation on her forehead descending to the bridge of her nose. There were three or four lines down each side of her nose. Two tattoo lines were curved along her cheeks. Below her full lower lip were seven or eight vertical lines down her chin and she had a slight cleft on her lower chin. I was told that she had some intricate tattoo designs on her arms, though I never saw them. Father Tardif heard that she had been a very good hunter as a younger person. I was especially flown to Holman Island to sculpt Kalvak's bust because she was considered an exceptional artist. However this commission proved to be one of my most trying, chiefly on account of her overindulged grandchild and his aversion to me, an intruder in his domain."

"It was around Easter 1955 that I first met George Washington Porter in Gjoa Haven. I was working with the X-ray survey team from Edmonton on our annual checkup tour. George was the general factotum around the settlement and spoke good English. It wasn't too often that we had time to sit around and chat and indeed it was rare to find a native who knew any English.

"After we had completed our work, we stopped at George's for a quick cup of tea before winging our way back to our pied à terre in Cambridge Bay on Victoria Island. One of the doctors on the team was an old friend of George's and they got into an animated conversation about the whaling industry and conservation on the Alaskan coast. It was only then that I realized that old George was a man of varied and unusual experience. Unhappily, our pilot announced that we must leave right away because the sun was getting pretty low. My appetite was really whetted to hear more of his adventures and I made a

George Washington Porter (Oloogak), Gjoa Haven, NWT, 1974

mental note to look up this man if I was ever to return. Almost twenty years passed before I got a commission to sculpt a bust of him in 1974.

"As it was midsummer, the school was vacant and I arranged to use it. It was really the only suitable place to work in, and I bunked in there too. It was a very short walk from George's house and, through him, I arranged to have my meals at his son's house which was also close by.

"Normally, George was a most gregarious and garrulous person, but it took two sittings before he got into his usual talkative stride. I was itching to get him to tell me his story. I am sure that he had told it many times, for, once he started, he rambled on at length, giving me details from his youth in Alaska until the recent past in Gjoa Haven.

"He was the child of a Scottish-American whaling captain of the same name and an Alaskan Inuit woman. His father had come from Peterhead in Scotland to New Bedford, Massachusetts, to work as a whaler. Later he moved to San Francisco, still in whaling. He soon became a captain in his own right and his work took him much farther north. George was born on one of his father's ships.

"His formal schooling was very haphazard, but his apprenticeship on whalers with his father and later, as captain of other ships, was very productive and satisfying to his rugged nature. He whaled in Beaufort Sea, Smokey Mountain and Nelson Head, stayed at home for awhile, and then went off again to Point Barrow, Alaska.

"George Senior used to put in at Herschell Island where the whaling fleet frequently harboured. George's first few years were spent in that vicinity and in Point Barrow. Later they all moved to Anderson River, some 300 miles east, where George had his very first schooling and when he was about nine they moved back to Herschell Island.

"While his father was captaining the *Beluga,* George's parents felt that he should have more schooling and decided to leave him at Unilaska to attend the Methodist-Episcopal Home for boys and girls. Part of their tuition was given in service; the youngsters worked on the home's small farm, and they fished and then salted the catch for winter use in the home.

"It was at Herschell Island that he met the man whom his father had talked about so much, Vilhjalmur Stefansson. Porter senior was an old friend of Stefansson and in his book *My Life with the Eskimos,* he writes about this friendship. Stefansson "became" an Inuk, living the traditional life and experiencing all the moments of joy and sorrow, the lean years and the fat years.

"Another famous explorer whom George met shortly after this was the Norwegian, Raoul Amundsen, the first in the world to navigate the northwest passage.

"His apprenticeship on whalers served him well, for he worked on quite a few whaling ships. He proudly said that when he was eighteen, he was a real salt

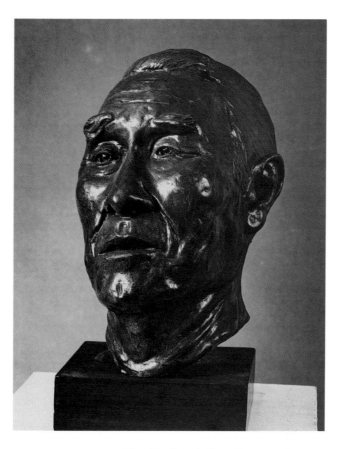

and went on the *Elvira* which was also a trading vessel. He really enjoyed this life but by about 1913 whaling was slowing down. Spending so much time at sea was lonesome and very isolating, making him rather restless. This isolation kept him in ignorance of the First World War. Going into Point Barrow the next year, he saw some movie shorts about the war in Europe. He and some of his adventurous friends decided to join up for war service. They had hardly got into uniform when the armistice was signed, so George went right back to whaling and trading.

Ikey Bolt, Coppermine, NWT, 1974

"With whaling dying out, trading seemed to be the way to go. The Hudson's Bay Company more or less dominated trade in the Northwest Territories. However, he decided to join a rival company, the Canadian Alaska Trading Co., working for them for five years in Vancouver. When this company folded its operations, George decided to join the Royal Canadian Mounted Police to serve on their schooner as a special constable. This was the famous schooner, *St. Roch*, which sailed from west to east through the Northwest Passage in 1941-42. George said that he piloted it for a little over a year. Later he went on *Tudlik*, the schooner owned by Stephen Angulalik, from Perry River to Herschell Island to collect furs. He went on to work for the Hudson's Bay Company in 1942, the first two years as a clerk and for twenty - three years alone in charge of a post, and retired in 1967.

"In my travels all over the arctic for many years, I have talked to many of the old-timers and am so often greatly impressed by their feats of endurance and bravery. Their songs are left unsung, but we owe them so much. Oloogak's bronze is in the Prince of Wales Northern Heritage Centre in Yellowknife.

"On a trip to Yellowknife in 1974, I met Dr. Hugh Rose, an ophthalmologist. He showed considerable interest in my sculpting and head hunting. While talking about some of the more interesting characters who had posed for me, he said that Ikey Bolt was coming to town the next day for an examination and to have a new glass eye made. I had heard of Ikey and was anxious to meet him.

"He was born in Point Hope, Prince of Wales Island, in Alaska, June 4th, 1894. When he was nineteen, he got a job on one of Stefanson's schooners on a trip down the southwest coast to Vancouver. During his association with the explorer, he made quite a few trips with him by dog team. Ikey eventually settled down in Coppermine with his wife, Edna, where they were highly respected. He was a storekeeper for many years, a trader and a lay reader in the Anglican Church. Edna was the daughter of the legendary Christian Klengenberg, who was nicknamed Sally. Klengenberg came to the north with the whalers, and when whaling died out, stayed and established himself as a successful trader. Ikey taught school in Coppermine and was a catechist in the Anglican church for many years until his failing eye sight made this impossible.

"Dr. Rose suggested I come to his clinic the following day and he would introduce me to Ikey. That evening I spent with an old friend, Ernie Lyall, at his home. Ernie and Ikey had not seen each other for many years so I suggested he join us.

"When Dr. Rose was inserting various lenses into the empty frame and asking if "this one is better than the last," Ikey would reply, "No, I can't see Ernie," or, "Oh, I've lost my friend," and, "I've found him again." After the session, we all sat around in the doctor's waiting room while I showed them photos of my sculptures. Both of them knew many of the sitters well. I then asked Ikey if he would pose for me and he agreed to do so. We got along splendidly and, because of his age, eighty, and his very poor eyesight, I decided to take him in hand. I took him by taxi up to Akaitcho Hall where I had a suite. We had lunch there and I got him to lie down for a rest. He wanted to do a bit of shopping, so we taxied down town and he purchased a few items. Then we went out to Imperial Optical where he got two pairs of spectacles. At 5:00 PM he had an appointment with Desmond Grant, the oculist, who had been making a plastic eye for him. Des ground and polished the eye until it was comfortable and fitted perfectly. Ikey left for Coppermine early the next morning and I followed on the 11:15 airplane.

"In a couple of days, the modelling was completed, and I began making moulds, and later cast a positive of the bust in plaster of Paris. My audience, young and old, had never witnessed such a procedure, and they were really excited as they watched the 'reincarnation.' Ikey's bronze head is now in the Prince of Wales Northern Heritage Centre in Yellowknife. He was a very fine gentleman. He died in 1981."

"I went to Fort MacPherson with a commission to sculpt Chief Johnny Kay and I had arranged to stay with The Reverend Mr. Simon. James Simon was an

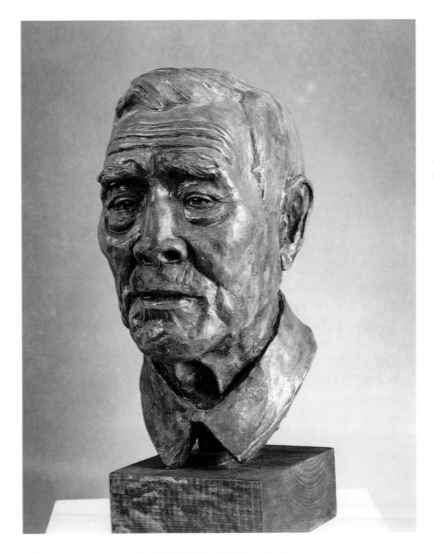

Chief Johnny Kay,
Fort MacPherson, 1976

Anglican minister and his wife was a dedicated social worker. When I stayed with them in 1976, they were probably in their late sixties. Their modest house had several bedrooms, separated by partitions but no doors. My bunk was curtained off in the hallway.

"I had a pleasant meeting with the Chief and he agreed to pose for me. News got around that the fellow who got off the plane was going to do the Chief's picture and of course everyone was curious to witness this unusual event. Drinking was a very serious problem in that settlement at the time and, an hour after the liquor store opened, it was not unusual to see a few men staggering by in the street, and sometimes a woman as well. I found the sight sad and shocking.

"The Chief was very co-operative. I had already built up an armature and was ready to start modelling him. He sat for an hour or so then had to go out for a bit. I continued to work checking my measurements which I had previously taken; soon a man came in who was quite inebriated. He sat alongside me, then stretched out on the sofa, fell asleep and promptly slid onto the floor. He was curled up around my feet when, after a while, he awakened, looked up into the Chief's clay face and stared. With a great shout he called out "Holy Geez, I t'ought I seed a ghost!" He pulled himself together and left. This unnerved me and I decided that I needed a break and took a short walk.

"The Chief never locked his door and, when I returned, I found two very inebriated men partially sprawled across the table surrounded by empty beer cans. They started questioning me: "Who sent you here to do this? How much are you going to pay Johnny for his time? How much are you going to make out of it?" It didn't take me long to decide to take up my armature and leave.

"Arriving at the Simons' house, I found it full of little children. Several sleeping bags were laid out and Mrs. Simon was busy cooking supper for them all. She told me that the youngsters always came over to her house for fear of being hurt by their inebriated parents. This apparently happened every time the liquor store got a shipment, when every car or truck in the settlement was hired to carry loads of beer home.

"The chief gave me some good sittings, and I finished the bust. The bronze is in the Glenbow Museum. It was a sad settlement and I did not linger. The Simons were a magnificent couple, who tried hard to improve living conditions there."

Harold arrived in Grise Fiord, Ellesmere Island, in 1978, on a hair-raising flight from Resolute through fog, cloud and drizzle in a Twin Otter filled with nine children, nine adults and an enormous quantity of baggage. After a very dicey landing, and a noisy welcome among natives, mountain climbers and settlement personnel, someone noticed him, a stranger in their midst, and asked if he had brought his own food with him. The supply ship was late, and there was practically nothing left on the shelves at the store. Keeping fed was a constant challenge throughout his stay.

The assignment was to sculpt the head of Philapusie, the oldest Inuit in the settlement. Many years before, Philapusie lived in Port Harrison, Hudson's Bay, where he was said to have been a vigorous and adventurous fellow, a good hunter and fisherman.

In 1953, the federal government, because there was insufficient game to sustain the growing Inuit population, relocated seven families from Port Harrison in northern Quebec to the high arctic in Resolute Bay and Craig Harbour (now Grise Fiord), more than 2,000 kilometers north. This has since become a controversial subject because it has been revealed that the government's motive was not just to alleviate population pressure on the supply of game. A key factor in the decision was the perceived need to promote Canadian sovereignty in the arctic by establishing permanent settlements of Inuit as far north as possible. The government also hoped to reduce the cost of providing relief supplies and services. Although their letters home speak of plentiful game, the consequences

Philapusie and
Annie Novalinga,
Grise Fjord, 1978

were apparently horrendous for the relocated families. They were separated from loved
ones, some for decades, some permanently, and left to struggle in an unfamiliar and
hostile environment with virtually no support.

After ten years in Grise, Philapusie attempted to return to Port Harrison, renamed
Inukjuak, to find that most of his old friends had died or moved away. The younger
generation were not enthusiastic about his plan to settle, and he went back to Grise to
share his home with his daughter and family. In fact, his house was probably the most
comfortable in Grise.

> "His one compensation was that, having a bad heart, he had had a pacemaker
> installed, and this excited much curiosity and sympathy. On his regular visits to
> Montreal to "recharge his batteries" he was impressed by the grandeur of city
> life and the many large fine houses and thousands of shiny new cars. He said
> that in these homes, "the wind didn't go through the cracks in the walls."
>
> "He spoke some English, though sometimes when I spoke to him, he put his
> hands over his ears, indicating he was deaf to the English language. However,
> when it was to his advantage, he always managed to grasp the meaning of a
> story. He was very jolly, smiling a lot; he apparently got a bang out of life.

"Annie, his wife, was more serious, and seemed a shadow in his background.

She baked the best bannock in the arctic, as far as I was concerned. The fact that there was nothing on the co-op shelves for me to eat besides Pilot biscuits (hard tack) may have influenced my opinion. She often sprinkled raisins in the dough, and when she broke the ring into pieces, I unashamedly took the largest.

"As usual when I am arranging for a sitting, I showed Philapusie my album of my work, with photos of my bronzes, and some of me and my subject with the model, which helps convey what I am after. As he was looking through the album, he came upon a familiar face and got very excited, calling to his wife and children to look at the photo, saying, *"Najagi vara, najagi vara, najaga!"* I asked Sarah what the excitement was about and she replied that Phil said that the photo was of his sister, Elizabee. I said this was quite impossible, because I had done the head in 1955, thousands of kilometers away, down in Port Harrison. She said that was where Phil had come from, twenty-five years ago. Phil was ecstatic and called in all the neighbours to see the photo. I was delighted that he recognized the likeness I had made, and our friendship was cemented. I was practically adopted into the family.

"After I had modelled him, and made the moulds, I cast a positive of his head, and shellacked it with brown shellac. When I showed it to him, he was taken aback at the dark brown colour, and exclaimed, "I am not a black man!" However, he was extremely pleased with it, and the whole settlement came in to see it.

"The next day I was to leave, and I was up bright and early for my flight. The Department of Transport man called out to me as I walked up to the landing pad, "Forget it, a storm is coming up, the flight has been cancelled; you'll be here at least another week." My first thought was food! The supply ship had still not arrived, and the co-op was barer than ever, carrying a few jars of jam, jelly and ketchup; not very nourishing.

"One of the mountain climbers who were waiting in the settlement for the right weather conditions for climbing in the Macinson Mountains was Murray Wallace of Banff. I bought a quantity of granola, nuts, raisins and dates from him and his fellow mountaineers, so I was able to stave off starvation, though I did lose some weight.

"My time in the arctic was very precious, so I decided I must take the opportunity to do another head. I had my clay and sufficient plaster of Paris; my association with Phil and Annie was already well established, and Annie's bannock was an additional attraction: she agreed to sit, and my stranding in Grise was very fruitful. I came home with two portraits, the bronzes of which are in the Prince of Wales Northern Heritage Centre in Yellowknife."

"In 1979 I had a commission from the Prince of Wales Northern Heritage Centre to do a portrait bust of Harriet Gladue in Fort Norman. Harriet was born in

Fort Norman (Kelly Lake) on February 23, 1897. Her father Samuel Horasy and her mother Louisa were Slavey Indians. When she was sixteen, she married her first husband, Albert White, who was chief for ten years. Her second husband was Noel Gladue, a Cree. They were married on December 26, 1903.

"Harriet acted as midwife to hundreds. She told me some harrowing tales of when she was called to help at difficult births, often during a blizzard. She had to snowshoe through deep drifts and through tangled bush to find the cabin or tent. Frequently little or no preparation had been made. Intuition guided her when she went to such a home where even the bare necessities were lacking. She usually brought a packsack of extra blankets and some clean linen. Harriet was a real heroic pioneer in her profession. It is a pity that she was not honoured with the Order of Canada. I sadly regret that I never suggested this be done.

"We corresponded for many years, and in her last Christmas letter, when she was ninety-six, she told me that she was giving up sewing. For many years Harriet made my buckskin gloves from the hides of moose which Noel had shot, smoked and tanned. She was now enjoying daily visits of her grand and great-grandchildren and she was a great favourite in the community. Her husband Noel died in November 1985 and Harriet passed on in Fort Norman in November 1993. She was truly a wonderful woman. Her bronze bust is in the Heritage Centre in Yellowknife."

Harriet Gladue, Fort Nelson, NWT, 1979

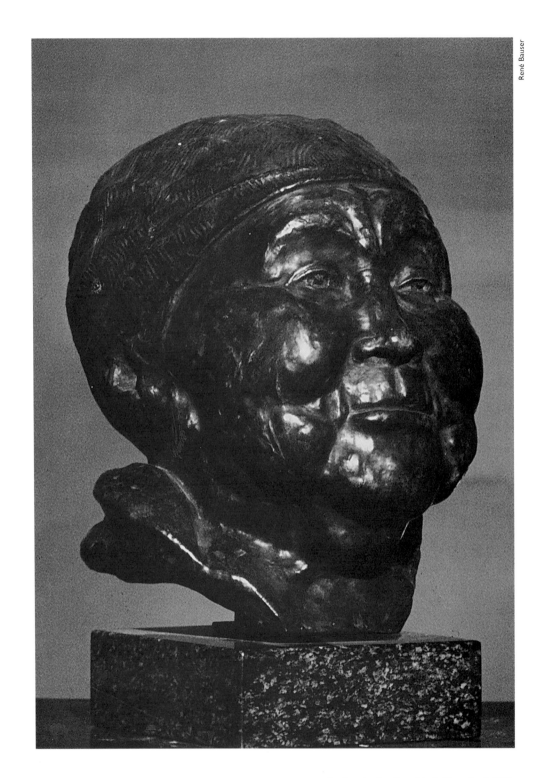

Annikatrina Josefsen, Nuuk, Greenland, 1975

Closing the Circle: Greenland and Arctic Siberia

Travel has been an important part of Harold Pfeiffer's life. His affection for people of all kinds, and his curiosity about their ways and means of getting through life, have led him to South Africa, South America, the Caribbean, Europe and the Soviet Union, and five times around the world on cruise ships. A trip to Greenland in 1974, where Harold completed eight portraits of Greenland Inuit, added a link in the circumpolar chain.

The most usual jumping-off place to Greenland is Copenhagen where the jets fly to Sondre Strom Fjord airport. The capital, Godthaab (pronounced Godhope) had a population of about 9,000 people, mostly Danish administrative personnel. (Yellowknife, the capital of the Northwest Territories has some 15,000 inhabitants.) Since the independence of Greenland from Denmark, Godthaab has acquired a new name, Nuuk.

There are only two airports on this, the world's largest island. The only one of consequence, allowing the big jets from Copenhagen to land, is the base built by the U.S. during World War II at Sondre Stromfjord. This is at the end of the longest fjord about a quarter of the way up the island about 120 miles in from the west coast. The ice cap is only a few miles away, an awe-inspiring sight.

113

Helicopters, small ships and boats are the only means of travel among the very scattered inhabited settlements. Jets and other planes can navigate in most weather conditions but proper runways are essential for takeoff and landing. A helicopter pilot must be able to see the ground and a few hundred yards around him. The travel brochures do not tell you that fog and sudden snow storms may ground you for days.

"When we arrived from Copenhagen on a beautiful day in early August, we found the hotel crowded with people who had been stranded for a few days because the 'copters were grounded in Nuuk and Sukkertoppen. There was heavy fog in both places. Every day the jets brought in dozens of passengers, mostly Greenlanders and Danes returning from summer vacations in Denmark. The planes returned to Europe almost empty. I was lucky to get away in four days.

"There were lots of interesting people to talk to, botanists, archaeologists, mining and oil men, as well as a group of Danish and Greenlandic teachers,

Harold with four of his Greenland bronzes, 1975

the Director of Education for Greenland, and the Provost of the Lutheran Church for all of Greenland. The U.S. airbase was rather sad looking. The well-kept but mostly vacant buildings offered certain comforts to strangers grounded by the elements. A movie house showed some sleepers and if you were lucky, a fairly recent movie, and the prices were reasonable. Although heavily subsidized by the parent government, prices were generally very high. It was quite a shock to visit the supermarkets in Godthaab to find people avidly buying eggplants, avocados, kiwi fruit, asparagus, melons, peaches, pears, grapes, caviar *en masse*, and even lobster tails.

"There was absolutely nothing to do at the base but go for walks. Sometimes these were rewarded by the sight of reindeer and muskoxen as was my good fortune one day. The silt and ground rock is so fine that each step disturbs a cloud of it. On return it was necessary to take a shower. My stay in Greenland was a most rewarding and happy one. The people were kind and generous.

"The Government has spent hundreds of thousands renovating and restoring the historic homes and buildings in Nuuk. I was immensely impressed by the beautiful home in which the Governor and Mrs. Hans Lassen lived. It was furnished with many fine family antiques and paintings. Also the home of the Chairman of the Provincial Council, Pastor Lars Chemnitz. This magnificent large house has stone walls three feet thick and is a veritable museum full of historically interesting prints, maps, paintings and memorabilia of Old Greenland.

"It was my first time in Greenland, and not having any specific individuals to sculpt, I wandered around Godthaab wide-eyed, looking for subjects to sculpt. Passing a large institutional building, I noticed a group of old ladies sitting on a bench, sunning themselves. Three or four of them were listening to a jolly old lady telling a story. They were all laughing. I walked on, but there was something magnetic about that woman. My first impressions of her happy face caught me, and I thought a bust of her would be impressive.

"The next day I went down to talk to the matron of the home and it was arranged; for the next few days Annikatrina Josefson sat for me. Though we could not speak each others' language, we both got a lot of fun out of it, especially when her friends came to criticise my work.

"I was staying with Dr. John Jensen, the Director of Education, and he kindly came over several times to interpret for us. Doing Annikatrina's portrait was a good introduction. Word spread, and journalists came to speak to me.

"Hans Lygne, an artist and writer, suggested a number of subjects to me, and I went around looking them up. I found Judithe Henrikson myself in church in Fiskenaeset, and I met Lars Rasmussen in Godthaab Fjord.

"On Thursday, October 3, at the heliport in Godhaab, the weather looked fair and a patch of blue showed through the clouds. The first stop on our way to Sondre Stromfjord was to be Sukkertoppen (Sugarloaf), forty-five minutes airtime from Godthaab. This is where they refuel for the longer flight to Sondre Stromfjord where we were to take the SAS jet to Copenhagen. The weather was quite good the first half hour or so, then we got into a nasty fog and then a snow storm. To avoid the worst of the storm, we flew into fjords which seemed clear but, going around a bend, we found we were in a whiteout. The pilot had to retrace his way out. Trying a new route, we had the same experience and we seemed to be going around in circles, frequently not able to see in any direction; the 'copter would just have to fly upwards to avoid the rocks and peaks. The flying time was eating up fuel and although we got to within two air miles of Sukkertoppen, we just couldn't make it because of the storm. It was very frightening, especially when we saw the rotor blades spinning within a few feet of the cliffs and jagged mountain tops. I've had quite a few frightening experiences in my globetrotting but I must say that several times on this trip I felt that this was it and my number was about to be called.

"As our fuel ran short, the pilot tried to land us in some fjords where there were a few settlers, but he just couldn't get into them and we finally settled down on quite a nice level meadow at the end of a fjord, just as we ran out of fuel. Our pilot, Captain Nielsen, a Swede, who had more than eight years flying 'copters in the fjords, said afterwards that this was the first time he had experienced such a flight. The copilot, a Norwegian with five years on this route said the same thing. Their magnificent ability was tested and confirmed. He radioed our position to Godthaab and requested that fuel be sent out. There were no helicopters there at the time so they sent out petrol in a speed boat.

"We were only nineteen miles out from Nuuk but as the coast is full of islands and shoals, it took them about six hours to find us. By the time they arrived, our feet were very cold and we welcomed the hot coffee and sandwiches they brought. My heart went out to the boat's crew and our pilots and the mechanic when they unloaded the very heavy barrels of petrol off the deck into the tiny rowboat. Then there was the herculean job of lifting the barrels out of the boat on to the slimy seaweed-covered rock and rolling them up the bank and over and around rocks and boulders. We gave them a grateful welcome for their efforts.

"There was about four inches of wet snow on the ground when we landed. As we originally set out to fly from Sondre Stromfjord and on to Copenhagen on a jet that noon, we were not dressed for slush. Wind and sun melted it quite quickly. We were very glad to be able to get out and stretch. The ground was covered with heather and crowberrries; they are shiny black, the size of our wild blueberries, quite sweet and juicy and full of tiny seeds. Greenlanders and Danes make jam from them. Where there is soil in the meadows and up the mountainsides they grow profusely. The mountains are gorgeous and the scene changes very quickly. The landscape will be completely white and within a few hours, the sun and wind will melt the snow on the lower slopes and meadows, the grey rocks will be livened up by the lovely copper leaves of the crowberries, the yellow leaves of the blueberries and the orange-red of the creeping birch. The air is so unpolluted and the sky so beautifully blue, one can see for miles.

"The radio carried the news of our forced landing and when we returned to Nuuk, we were met by many concerned well-wishers. We were indeed grateful to our pilot who so skilfully manoeuvered our helicopter in many extremely tight spots."

A long-standing dream of Harold's was to go to the most northerly part of Eastern Siberia, on the coast of the Bering and Chukchi Seas, where a very small group of Yuits have survived for thousands of years. The Yuit peoples originated here, later to spread across the arctic to Alaska, the Canadian north, and eventually to Greenland. Having sculpted native people in all these places, he wanted to complete the circumpolar link with some portraits from their ancestral homeland.

Getting permission from the U.S.S.R. was no easy task. After fourteen years of repeated requests through External Affairs, it was not until a visit to his Ottawa studio by Madame Shevardnadze with Maureen McTeer in 1987, that the wheels were really set in motion.

Eventually he received a formal invitation from the Union of Soviet Artists and the Soviet government, and went to Siberia as their guest in 1988. He finished eight portrait busts and had many adventures.

"Stuart Hodgson was particularly keen that I make this trip, as was our Ambassador in Moscow, Mr. Robert Ford. However, the idea was all but abandoned. I credit Ms. Maureen McTeer, wife of Joe Clark, former Prime Minister and Secretary of State, for activating the trip.

"Ms. McTeer was very interested in art and when Mr. Eduard Shevardnaze and his wife came to Ottawa, Ms. McTeer was her hostess during the visit and asked if she might bring Madame Shevardnaze and her entourage to my studio to see my sculptures. During her visit, Madame asked why I was so interested in native people and after showing her examples of the many different rugged types which I had sculpted in Alaska, the Northwest Territories and in Greenland, I said that my great ambition was to go to Northern Siberia to sculpt the last remaining group of the Inuits; the descendants of the original race. Remarking that mine was a collection of great historical importance and a national treasure, Madame agreed that including Siberians would be an important step in advancing glasnost. Ms. McTeer interjected that this would be an international gesture representing Alaska (U.S.A.), the Northwest Territories, Canada, Greenland (Denmark) and finally Siberia (U.S.S.R.).

"Shortly after this, I had several prominent Soviet artists and sculptors visit my studio as well as the ambassador and other diplomatic personages. Ms. McTeer pursued the idea with External Affairs and the trip was finally arranged. I received an invitation from the Union of Soviet Artists and the U.S.S.R. Government and went to Siberia as their guest in 1988. The Department of External Affairs paid some of my expenses. During my trip I was interviewed by five newspapers and several magazines. *Pravda* devoted two full columns to my enterprise, including my photograph. There were very few problems and no restrictions were imposed as to where I wished to go.

"Farley Mowat wrote before I left and told me that I would have a great time in Chokotka. That I did, and found so many similarities with our arctic, Alaska, Baffin Island and up in Ellesmere Island and Greenland. When I was sculpting in Uelen, some curious children would stand at the window and watch me modelling, but they would never venture into the studio uninvited. It was an exception when someone glanced at me as I walked down the road. After I had given away a few Canadian flag buttons to the children, the odd youngster would approach me in a friendly manner, obviously seeking a similar gift. I had brought along quite a supply of pins, lollipops and hard candy, but most in demand were the rubber dinosaurs, which were apparently a novelty.

"Everywhere I went, word had been sent ahead that a VIP artist from Canada was to visit their settlement and the administrator and some councillors were always awaiting us as we stepped off the plane or helicopter. We were always ushered into a meeting room where sandwiches and vodka was offered to us. My companions were delighted, but as I am not much of a drinker, it was a bit embarrassing for me.

"Of course, in the Soviet Union, artists, like authors, were VIPs and many privileges were bestowed on them. Hence, they always managed to find the odd bottle of vodka. I also learned that quite a few of them make their own liquor. Indeed, a judge who gave a dinner party for me in Magadan told me that he made his own wine, which we were drinking at dinner. There were continual toasts to me, which always had to be translated, which became a real embarrassment.

"Chokotka is so different from any of our arctic regions because there are many quite large industrial cities and many small towns, not just settlements as in our arctic. Magadan, our first stop, was a sprawling city of some 100,000 people. We were housed in a large three-storey building, on a slight hill, surrounded by a small park. Only government officials stayed here.

"It was nicely furnished in typical Russian Hotel style, very polished furniture, a sizeable dining room, several lounges, a TV area, a billiard and ping-pong room. For several days we were the only guests in the place, yet all our meals were prepared for us. They were standard and rarely varied, mostly cold-cuts and a lettuce and cucumber salad. One unusual thing: there were packages of cigarettes and small bars of chocolate laid out on a side board, free for the taking.

"Our bedrooms were small, with an attached bathroom, and as usual, the rubber stopper in the sink and bath were missing. This being my fourth visit to the Soviet Union, I came prepared, and brought along a small rubber ball, which covered up any size hole. A small fridge, a hot plate and a large combination clothes closet were supplied, with a glassed-in area for two plates, two cups and saucers, two glasses and some cutlery. These amenities were really appreciated when we wished to make up a snack. From here on, our accommodation became very much more rustic, until our final most northerly stop at Uelen and there, our "hotel" was the pits!

"To get to the settlement of Anadyr from the airport one can go on a ferry across the bay or drive on a long rough road, the ferry being quite a shortcut. When we arrived on the ferry, I think all the artists in the vicinity were there to meet us. There was great cheering when we got off. Yuri seemed to know most of them from when he worked up in Uelen years earlier. As is the custom of artists, our arrival was an excellent excuse to have a party. It started off as a dinner they cooked themselves, with a variety of spirits. Yuri and Serge, my interpreters, thoroughly enjoyed themselves, but because of the language barrier, I just had to smile and be an onlooker.

"I enjoyed Anadyr very much. It had quite an art colony and they gave me a fine studio to work in. I got along perfectly with the young sculptor, Yvan Melnikov, who was doing some excellent work there. I had a bit of trouble finding a suitable subject and finally suggested that we go to the old folks home and look them over. The matron brought me into the TV room where a group was watching the screen and I chose my man. I found a Yuit with good features and he was a most

118

Ayaya Tagyok,
Uelen, Siberia, 1988

119

agreeable sitter. He had been a sniper during the war and apparently was an excellent marksman and had received a medal for it. He was so animated when I listened to his story that his lines of joy and sorrow were clearly etched on his face, and I felt that I was able to capture some of his character. The matron arranged an empty room for me to work in and I had my meals there, so I did not waste much time. The old guy just would not admit that he was tired and let me have quite a few really long sittings. After finishing the modelling I brought it back to the studio and made moulds and finally the plaster cast. The other artists seemed to really like it too. Being a bit of a perfectionist, when I look over my finished plaster cast, I often feel that had I had another sitting with my subject, I could have improved the work.

"From my personal knowledge of having worked all around the circumpolar arctic rim, I was greatly impressed by the superiority of the artists in this small group. One man, Vladimir Praskov, who came from Magadan, asked me to pose and in an hour and a half produced a splendid sketch portrait.

"One of the artists was a well-known etcher, another, a graphic artist and illustrator. Yvan Melnikov was a young sculptor who had just received a special honour from Moscow which was also the cause of some celebration. At the end of the evening, I was presented with two paintings, an etching, a book with illustrations done by one of the artists and a small plaster figure of a Yuit woman by Melnikov. Their generosity was quite embarrassing and it was difficult for me to adequately show my gratitude. The following day, the graphic artist presented me with a book plate with my name on it, a drawing of a Billican holding a modelling tool in his hand. He had printed a few dozen. Everywhere I went, people presented me with autographed art books. One was a copy of Farley Mowat's People of the Deer in Russian. This is one place which will always have a particularly warm place in my memory.

"Our final destination was Uelen, the most notherly outpost on the northeast cost of Siberia. There is quite a concentration of the original Yuit people there. Because of the rocky terrain and the few people to service this far north, no airstrips had been built. Transportation is by helicopter or by boat. We would have had to wait for several days before the next 'copter left for Uelen. My visa did not officially permit me to go by boat or to visit some of the little settlements on the way to Uelen. However, my interpreter was a KGB fellow and as I discovered, had a good deal of clout in dealing with the many who felt that they were of some importance in the community. He arranged that we take the boat that was sailing at midnight. We were privileged to get the only cabin on board, sleeping four, in the prow. Because the sun was still on the horizon, I stayed up most of the night. We stopped at several small settlements while the crew unloaded supplies and the odd passenger boarded or left the ship. It was very rough and several passengers were very ill. Luckily I am a good sailor, having made many trips on

coastal freighters to Europe in all sorts of weather. We saw many icebergs and great pans of ice floating by. A few whales spouted nearby. The only ships we saw were a diesel fuel ship and a coal freighter.

"We arrived at Uelen about midnight. There was no wharf so the ship just ploughed its nose into the pebble bank, keeping its engines running ahead until the tide changed. There was no one to meet us; apparently there had been a slip-up somewhere. Yuri, the master carver who accompanied us, got off to investigate where we were to sleep. We stood on the beach for over an hour and a half before arrangements could be made. People had to be awakened and two rooms had to be cleaned up and prepared. Finally Yuri turned up with a couple of not-too-happy men and we were led up a path over clinkers and coal to the one and only roadway. We walked about a quarter of a mile to the end of the road to our lodging house. There had been some trouble with the electrical plant and there was no electricity. The cleaning up was done by the light of a flashlight. Although it was about 1:30 AM and fairly bright outside, indoors was really dark. A man opened the door to my "cell" and I tripped over a curl of worn linoleum. When my eyes focused on the interior, I was surprised.

"The room was about 6' x 14', containing a narrow bunk, a fridge, two children's chairs, a small table, a phone, and a mirror hung so high up that I could only see to comb my hair. There was a hot plate, a kettle, two cups and saucers and a soup bowl, but no cutlery. They never seem to have any knives, and the forks and spoons are made of aluminum. A radio was screwed to the wall and seemed to emit only rock 'n roll day and night unless strangled. Next door was the two-holer. One does not sit on it, one squats. The filth and stench of these open toilets was really disgusting, especially when the wind blew our way.

"I can understand why this expedition of mine was delayed because, in this remote area, there were no foreign visitors and one had to make do, or else. I also came across several other filthy sights in the school where in the toilets people did not aim properly and no one seemed to bother cleaning up.

121

"Yuri and Serge were ushered down the hall to a double room which was undoubtedly the best in the place. Like so many rooms in Russian homes, two of the walls had oriental rugs hung on them and there was a scatter rug between the beds. They had a fridge, two glasses, two cups and saucers, two soup bowls, two plates, two forks and two spoons. Further down the hall was a small alcove in which were two sinks with running water, one of which occasionally had warm water. Opposite the sinks were two huge metal drums supposedly holding drinking water. I took the wooden lid off one and found the interior almost completely corroded and a deposit of rust-covered the water. I chose to boil the water from the other taps and did not worry about the few odd specks of unknown origin in it.

"Not knowing the language was a great disadvantage. The scarcity of food was frequently a problem. We ate our meals at the canteen down the road. It was well run, but the menu was either fish or reindeer meat and servings were not plentiful. Many of the women were away on vacation, hence the majority of the patrons were men. About seventy-five percent of the population were Yuit, twenty percent Chukotkans and the rest Russians. The canteen was open for only an hour at noon and at six o'clock when the food was served. One could sit around for a bit, chatting, but then they locked up. On two occasions a note was tacked on the door announcing that the canteen was closed for lack of food, but that they would be opening at next meal time. Warned by this, I bought some buns and a few things which I kept in my little fridge. One weekend I really was stuck; the canteen was closed, as was the only shop selling food. Luckily, Yuri knew some of the natives and he brought me over to a friend's apartment and they fed me some bologna and a sort of bannock. Then the woman cooked me a small can of boiled rice to take home. Two men in the next room kindly gave me a large slice of salmon, which they had cooked. I was indeed grateful. Yuri and Serge apparently knew of such shortages and when I got back to the "hotel" found that they had managed to acquire several tins of caviar and some bread. The KGB boys enjoyed many privileges.

"The main industry employed several dozen talented artists and carvers. This was a factory where master carvers produced a series of ivory carvings which were judged by a committee. The finest and most marketable were used as samples for the men and women to reproduce.

"Many years previously, Yuri had been in charge here and supplied many exquisite carvings which were copied or which inspired others to design and carve. When I was first shown through the factory museum, I saw many of Yuri's originals, as I did at the museum in Magadan, and I was impressed by his outstanding talent. There were quite a few women employed making articles in leather, mostly of reindeer hide. It all reminded me of scenes of mass production I had seen in China and Japan. The factory was a large three storey building with many large rooms for eight or ten carvers, each at their own work table, all sorts of power tools, drills etc., and individual fume and dust collectors. Some of the more prominent carvers had their own private rooms to work in.

"One room held piles of walrus tusks. There were men grading them. They first used coarse rasps, removing irregularities on the tusks, then passed them on to others who used files and various grades of sandpaper until finally they were burnished with high-speed cotton polishers.

"Some of the largest and best examples were given to the men or women who specialized in engraving arctic landscape scenes or bears, kayaks, komatik and dog teams. Only a master carver would design and complete a carving. The other artists specialized in carving reindeer, or just antlers, polar bears, or dog teams in many configurations. Others assembled and completed the finished carvings.

"I was amazed at the great pile of tusks in the factory. It reminded me of an elongated photo which I saw in the judge's house in Magadan, about eighteen inches high by twelve or fourteen feet long, of a scene taken along the northeast coast of Siberia, showing about 40,000 walrus basking in the sun.

"As many of the carvers were out on vacation, I was given a small studio to myself. Radios were going at a great rate, mostly rock and heavy metal, which nearly drove me mad. When some of them were out for coffee-break, I frequently toned down nearby radios which helped a little to preserve my sanity. The hunch-backed artist Edward Tagenko in the studio next to mine set up his easel in the hall way and did a portrait of me sculpting the man who was posing for me. It turned out to be remarkably good. I had my interpreter ask him if he would sell it to me but he would not. However, when I was leaving, the director gave a little farewell party for me, presenting an autographed ivory carving to me, and my neighbour presented the charcoal sketch to me also. I gave the hunch-backed artist my most treasured red and white hockey tuque and scarf. He rolled the drawing up so that it would be easy for me to carry. He was overjoyed and I was very happy. Several of the others gave me small gifts and books. I was, as always, impressed by their great generosity. I had been told that on no account should I offer them any money for services rendered, so I brought along quite a collection of tee shirts, scarves and tuques to give away, and several bags of assorted toys for the youngsters as well as maple leaf pins.

"Time was most precious to me, and so I chafed at the generous hospitality offered to me in each settlement. As I am naturally gregarious, enjoying parties and meeting people, it really hurt having to resist the many temptations which presented themselves daily. I worked all day, and often until midnight. At that time of the year the sun was always shining so I had quite good light to work with. However, on arriving home, I usually found someone using both sinks doing their washing or a couple of men gutting their fish; blood and guts everywhere! Then they would hang the fish out on a line by their windows to dry in the wind and sun. I must say they always apologised, and they cleaned up their mess before they left.

124

Tatooed woman, Inchun, Siberia, 1988

"I was always on the lookout to find an old lady with traditional tattoo marks on her face, and finally found a jolly old soul on the supply boat taking us from Providenya to Uelen. The Inuit women in Canada who were tattooed in their youth have all passed away. On my final day, walking out to the landing pad to take the 'copter to Sereniki and home, I passed three old ladies with tattoo marks on their faces. I stopped and showed them my camera but they covered their faces and walked on. I only wish that I had seen them earlier and had my interpreter handy to ask their permission to have one of them pose for me.

"One of my greatest concerns on my expeditions is packing and transportation of my supplies and my precious finished work. Having travelled and worked in some very remote areas of Alaska, the N.W.T., Greenland and in Africa, packing is always my major problem. I have a collection of tall empty chlorine carton-drums which are strong and light. Signs like "Handle With Care" or "Fragile" mean little to many people; in fact, sometimes it seems, to some handlers, they mean, "Throw, boys, throw." However, the drums can take a beating, and if they are properly packed, things travel quite safely.

"The drums are light until I fill them with my sculpting tools, armatures, plasticine, wax, liquids to make styrofoam or foam rubber and heavy plaster of Paris. Absolutely everything required must be included, for no shopkeeper in these areas has ever heard of art supplies. My hosts, the Union of Soviet Artists, had assured me that I could find everything which I would require in Magadan, Siberia's largest southern city. The plasticine they had was of a different consistency than I was used to and it was a very dark grey colour. Luckily, I had brought along some thirty pounds of my own which I used throughout the expedition. I also collected about 100 lbs. of plaster of Paris. Upon leaving Uelen, I gave the dark grey plasticine from Magadan to the artists in the School. Now my drums would be a smidgen lighter.

"Upon alighting from our plane or helicopter, the problem of carrying these heavy drums and our personal bags was always quite a headache. There were no porters, so we always had to manage the best way we could. Sergei and Yuri had to make several trips each to carry the drums. Sergei had been in the army and had picked up quite a collection of army slang. I was always amused when upon looking at our pile of luggage being unloaded from the plane, he would say "Those God-damn fucking crates!" Yuri did not know a word of English, but before we left, he had acquired three words: "Those fucking drums!" Yuri was one of the Soviet Union's most honoured artists and was a most pleasant and kind companion. Unfortunately the language was our great barrier. He frequently came around to watch me work and would sometimes help me in casting. Sergei was the complete opposite, no interest in art, a former army man, a chain smoker, employed to interpret for me and that was that.

"One day in Uelen, I saw a group of young sailors whom I had not seen before and started up a conversation with one who spoke quite good English. He was the first mate on the diesel supply ship and he asked if I would like to visit the vessel. I was so starved for English and the chance of a change of scene, I jumped at the idea. He said that he would send in a boat to collect me and my inter--preter at 8:00 PM. We had to walk for about two miles over pebble gravel to where the barge unloaded batches of about forty barrels of oil in steel drums. Very powerful tractors pulled them off the barge. The walking was like ploughing through soft, wet snow and it took us a good forty-five minutes to get to the barge. The officer in charge phoned on his walkie-talkie to the vessel that we had arrived. Apparently the first mate had retired early and had not advised any others that we might arrive as visitors. The captain was most cordial and said that he would send in a boat immediately for us.

"The captain spoke English and was very friendly. He showed us all over the ship and surprisingly asked if we would care to see a movie! It was a rather gruesome sad affair and he soon realized that we were not interested, so we retired to his cabin where a table was set out with cold cuts, home-made bread, biscuits and tea. My interpreter and my companion were both chain smokers. No smoking was permitted in the little theatre so they let loose in the cabin, for the captain provided them with boxes of cigarettes. I preferred the box of chocolates he offered us. We met the chief engineer, who was always referred to as "Grandfather," because he was the oldest man on the ship; sixty-five years old! Most of the lads seemed to be in their twenties and the captain was thirty-two. Most of the crew were from Vladivostock. It was a red-letter evening for me."

Upon his return to Ottawa, Harold had a visit from the Soviet ambassador, who viewed the Siberian portraits and expressed admiration for his work. His entry in Harold's guest book reads:

> Dear Harold:
> You look at the world with a warm eye and you reproduce it with
> a friendly hand.
>   A.A. Rodionov

Rodionov also noticed that Harold had a mask of Mikhail Gorbachev that he had begun while he was stranded by bad weather in Siberia, using Gorbachev's almost con-tinuous appearances on television as a model. The ambassador insisted he complete it as a full head, bringing him photographs of the Soviet leader to help him round out the portrait. Harold rarely worked from photographs, preferring the immediacy and intimacy of a live sitter, but as he was unlikely to ever to arrange a sitting with Gorbachev, he went along with the ambassador's enthusiasm.

Punch Dickens, Toronto, 1990

Northern Characters

The Inuit were not the only subjects that captured Harold Pfeiffer's imagination in the north. The history of the Canadian arctic is dotted with characters of mythic dimension, trappers and traders, bush pilots and visionary leaders who have shaped the modern north.

"I first met **Max Ward** in the spring of 1955 when I was a member of the X-ray team visiting remote settlements in the central and western arctic. Years later, in 1977, the Northwest Territories Government commissioned me to sculpt a portrait of him.

"I had been warned that if he agreed to pose for me it would be very difficult to pin him down for definite sittings. Many of my subjects have been very busy people who were available fairly regularly, but in Max's case, he seemed to have important meetings in Yellowknife, Edmonton, Calgary, Montreal or Toronto and even in England every few days. Even so, I was willing to take a chance.

"Our first sitting was in Yellowknife and he was leaving for the weekend to visit his wife and some guests at his camp some 115 miles further north at Red

Gerry Porter

Maxwell Ward, 1977

Rock Lake. He said that he could probably find a bit of time to pose for me up there and would I like to come along. Delighted, I said of course I would. Flying over miles of lakes, rivers and muskeg, we finally caught sight of his "camp." Surprise would hardly describe my feelings at the sight.

"Sitting out on a sandbar on the lake, I thought I must be looking at Disneyland. There were two huge circus tents made of bright canvas strips of white, red, yellow and green, like parents surrounded by their offspring, several smaller tents and a number of gaily painted toilet huts. To many of his guests who had never been in the high arctic, who might describe the terrain as somewhat drab, this scene was just a riot of colour and gaiety.

"This was not just a little weekend hideaway camp to get away from it all. For about a month every year it was a hive of activity. His guests for the first week were all VIPs from the airplane manufacturers he dealt with, presidents of banks, chairmen of great corporations. The following week he hosted another group which included many of the engineers and designers from the plane manufacturers' plants, with their wives, and the third week he entertained close friends and relatives. There were no children. His charming wife Marjorie was always busy being a warm hostess.

"For entertainment, he had six large boats with powerful outboard motors and a boathouse equipped with fishing rods, reels and lures, plus windbreakers for any who had not thought of bringing their own. When the guests came back from fishing, there was a smoke house handy where they could smoke their fish and pack them for shipping home.

"He imported a gourmet cook who always had trays of the most delectable canapés on a table laden with every sort of liquor and mixes and soft drinks. The chef was reputed to be the finest to be found in Edmonton. The proof of the pudding is in the eating, and I, who live for dessert, could not have been happier. Delightful box lunches were prepared for those who expected to be away for the day fishing. Dinner in the evening was always very jolly; most of the conversation beginning with tales of catches and the big one that got away.

"This all took place in late June, when the sun does not set for a few weeks. My first day I had several short sittings with Max and worked on the model after dinner for a bit. Along one wall in the main tent, where we lounged and had

Col. Patrick Baird, 1945

our meals, was a large plate-glass window about eight feet square facing the most attractive area on the lake. I left the plasticine model on the table by the window and talked to many of the guests who were curious to see a sculptor actually sculpting. Then we retired. There were two large dormitory tents for the men and two for the ladies. Alongside were two small buildings with sinks and showers for eight in each. Early in the year a very powerful grizzly bear, who couldn't contain his curiosity, had invaded the men's washroom and seeing a large steel hot water tank, attacked it with his forepaws, leaving great dents and deep claw marks in it.

"Max had decided to make some changes in one of the washrooms, and with one of his helpers ripped up the plumbing and some of the partitions. His helper left him to retire about 11:30. I slept in the men's dormitory in a bed alongside Max's bed. I was too excited to sleep and wondered when Max would tire of his work. Two, three, four o'clock and still the sound of nails being pulled; doesn't he ever get tired? I knew he had to talk to one of his pilots at 6:00 AM before he flew off to Yellowknife; when would he quit?

"He finally came in about 4:30 and was up at 5:45 and off to the dock to talk to his pilot. I dressed and we both went in to the dining tent for an early breakfast. Directly after eating, Max continued working on the washroom. Extraordinary energy! Some time later, he moved his camp further up the lake, below the cliffs of Red Rock.

"Going over to do some more work on my model, I touched it lightly and, to my great horror, found that the hours in the sun during the night had softened it to the consistency of soft butter. How could I cool it quickly without damaging it?

"The galley was in an adjoining tent and I asked the chef if I could put it in his large restaurant-size fridge. It was just crammed full of perishables, but he had an idea. A hole had been dug in the permafrost and a small cold room installed, a natural fridge. Very gingerly, I carried my precious armature down the icy steps to let it cool off. In an hour or so I was able to resume sculpting. Several guests thought that it was a splendid likeness, but I prevailed upon Max to let me have another sitting in Edmonton the following week. We had about a half-hour sitting there and I righted a few little details.

"With a 'PLEASE DO NOT DISTURB' sign on the door, I made the moulds and cast a plaster positive in the bathroom of my hotel room. This sort of activity is generally frowned upon by hotel management, but after I had tidied up my mess, no one was the wiser.

"I have a great deal of admiration for Max Ward. His is one of Canada's great success stories. Here was a young dedicated flyer, starting off as a fearless bush-pilot flying into the unknown north mostly by the seat of his pants; no reliable maps, no charts. A man with a great companion, his wife Marjorie. Under often appalling difficulties he built a great aviation empire in Wardair. Among some of the many honours which he has received is the Order of Canada. The bronze of him is in the Aviation Wing of the Prince of Wales Northern Heritage Centre in Yellowknife."

132

"Born July 12, 1912 in Newmarket, England, **Patrick Baird** became an educator, arctic explorer, glaciologist and an author. In the 1940s and 1950s he directed the office of the Arctic Institute in Montreal. During 1945 and 1946 he was the moving force in organizing the 'Operation Muskox' which was an exercise testing equipment for military purposes in the arctic. In 1955, he was awarded the Founder's medal from the Royal Geographical Society in London. I sculpted his bust in 1945 and it is in the McGill University collection. He was a professor there for some years. Colonel Baird passed away on July 1st, 1984."

"**Gus D'Aoust** was a trapper-trader from his late teens. He hunted and trapped with his brother, often in weather fit for no man. He was soft-spoken and had a care for both man and wildlife. I think of his great love and compassion for

Gus D'Aoust,
Yellowknife, NWT, 1977

133

Delphine, his beloved wife and partner for many years. Gus always had count-less chores to do around the cabin, chopping wood, repairing the dogs' harnesses, preparing the skins; just no end of jobs to be done.

"Delphine had gone out one day to check on her traps, and he became alarmed at the time she was away. Several times he looked out the frosted window but there was no sign of her. Pulling on his fur pants and parka, he was about to investigate. He heard the dogs whimpering and on opening the door, he saw Delphine lying haphazardly on the toboggan. The dogs had sensed trouble and had brought her home. Gus carried her into the cabin. She was unconscious and partially crippled with a stroke and could not speak. He described how he warmed her half-frozen body and brought her to life again. She could not communicate and there was no way of getting any assistance.

"When he finally got her to hospital in Yellowknife, he fed her and did every thing for her for over a year before she passed away. He relived the whole episode as he told it and I shed a few tears. Gus was a truly great person and I think Delphine was the same. When he was posing for me I set up my tape recorder while he told me stories about various animals which he had trapped or tried to trap, such as the wily wolverine.

"Gus' fascinating life is described in a biography entitled *Those Were the Days that I Lived and Loved*, by Alex Harpell. I had many delightful talks with him, and admired the man immensely. The bronze bust of him is in the Prince of Wales Northern Heritage Centre in Yellowknife."

Albert Faille,
Fort Simpson,
NWT, 1973

Albert Faille lived in the Northwest Territories for most of his life, having arrived in 1922, trapping near Tathlina Lake, eighty miles south of Fort Providence, until 1927. His partner did not enjoy the hardships of life in the north and departed, but Albert had heard the legend of the McLeod brothers' lost gold mine in the South Nahanni River valley, so there was no turning back for him. Every spring he would load up all his supplies and follow the Liard River from the Mackenzie to Nahanni Butte and enter the South Nahanni River. The Nahanni is an extremely fast and potentially treacherous river, especially in the approach to Virginia Falls, a 316-foot drop with the great cliffs on each side.

Albert would get as close to the falls as he could, beach and completely dismantle his boat, and portage all his food and gear and every plank of the boat to the river above the falls, a heroic job in itself. He then rebuilt the boat and continued upriver to one of the cabins he had built. In the early spring he would go down to Fort Simpson on the Mackenzie to sell his winter's catch of fur: marten, mink, lynx, fox, wolverine and the odd wolf pelt, and resupply for the following winter. He would stay in Fort Simpson for about three weeks, ample time to get his business done and do a little socializing.

134

One year, Albert Faille did not return. Edwin Lindberg, who as a boy lived at the Blackstone, eighty-five miles up the Liard from Fort Simpson, remembers: "The year he didn't come back, I believe, was late June 1942 when he left our home and said to Ole my father, 'Don't be surprised if I find gold this time. I'm going to keep poking around because I know just about where it is,' and with that he bid us goodbye.

"The next spring, late in May or early June, my brothers and myself would listen for the whine of Albert's four hp Johnson motor. He'd always bring us a large bag of chocolate bars just out of the goodness of his heart. Albert didn't show up that summer and late in the winter of '44, the RCMP searched the area where they thought his cabins were, but they couldn't find a trace of him. They assumed that he must have fallen through the ice or something of that nature."

In May of 1944, Albert was spotted walking along a sandbar in the river by two Fort Simpson trappers. He had run out of sugar, coffee and jam, but had several pounds of flour, some tea and several gunnysacks of dried sheep meat.

"Albert would have made it back to the so-called civilization without the help of the two trappers. He had lost all contact with the outside world when his battery pack for his radio went dead on him the first year that he was out on the trapline."

Faille worked as engineer on the *MV J.P. Murphy*, travelling with Dr. A. Truesdell who was magistrate, Indian Agent and doctor for the Liard-Mackenzie Region, from 1944 until 1950. When Truesdell retired, Albert went back to prospecting on the Nahanni. Again he was gone for almost two years. "Everyone in Fort Simpson thought he was a goner this time but he arrived back in good shape, both physically and mentally.

"Albert continued to search for gold on the Flat River, Nahanni River and many of the tributaries that flowed into them until 1967. He never found that rich vein of gold but he found many friends for he was a very generous and thoughtful fellow and everyone who knew him thought the world of him."

Bert Herridge was a prospector in the Yukon in his early days. He joined up at the beginning of the First World War and was severely wounded in battle. Invalided home, he became active in politics, first with the Liberal party,

Hon. H.W. Herridge, MP, Kootenay West, 1967

135

and then with the Co-operative Commonwealth Federation, which later became the New Democratic Party. He was elected MP for Kootenay West and was a popular and gregarious member of the House of Commons.

Known as "The Baron of the Kootenays," he was a tireless traveller in his constituency, though the challenge of getting over mountainous terrain by canoe and saddle horse was formidable, considering he had all but lost the use of a hand and an arm to his war wounds. His constituents were mostly Doukhobors, and they adored him because he took a genuine interest in their welfare.

Herridge's wife Ellen was a distant relative of the Pfeiffers, and during their time in Ottawa, they were Harold's frequent guests for Sunday tea. Herridge enjoyed talking as much as his host, and Harold delighted in his stories of adventure in the old days in the Yukon, of his Doukhobor constituents, whose unique form of political protest was to stand naked in groups, sometimes of fifty and more.

"On a visit to the Herridges in Nakusp, I met them in Nelson and we took the bus through the farmlands of the Doukobors, Bert at my side, introducing me to the countryside. As passengers got on the bus, they would doff their hats to him, and the conversation would flow: "And how is your daughter doing, did she get into that nursing school? And young Amos, how is he doing?" as if they were all old friends.

"When I had them over for tea, I always had a few of my younger friends in to meet them, for I knew they would enjoy Bert's sense of humour. One of his most popular stories was of a church garden party in the north, attended by all the important people of the community, including the ladies of the night, whose intimacy with some of the leading men was a well-known but unacknowledged fact. The atmosphere of the party was fraught with this unspoken awareness. He was very funny. People begged to be invited back. He was well respected in political circles too; Judy Lamarsh consulted him regularly."

Affectionately known as Father Mary, apart from his missionary duties **Father Guy-Marie Rosseliere** became intensely interested in arctic archaeology and was a great contributor in acquiring specimens and writing many papers on his findings. For many years he represented the Northwest Territories on the Historic Sites and Monuments Board. He passed away in a tragic fire that destroyed his parsonage and his church in Pond Inlet in 1994. The settlement was devastated. His passing left a great void in his church and in archaeological research in arctic Canada.

"I received a commission from the government of the Northwest Territories to do a portrait head of **J. Gordon Gibson**, who had been a valued councillor in the NWT government. When Commissioner Hodgson asked him to sit, he balked, saying he had "no time for such nonsense," but was eventually persuaded to agree under the condition that I do it on his yacht. What a wonderful opportunity! The yacht, the M/V *Maui Lu*, was the largest in Canada at the time; 132 feet long, and a beauty.

"I had heard that Gibson was a wealthy, gruff lumber baron and a very earthy character. I went aboard with some trepidation. He turned out to be colourful, congenial and co-operative. In free time we fished and gathered oysters along the B.C. coast, and I enjoyed his hospitality, and his other guests, immensely.

"Among the many kind and generous things he did, unbeknownst to most Vancouverites, was to invite groups of senior citizens for a day's picnic on his magnficent yacht. The galley was always well stocked and he personally saw to it that everyone had a great and memorable day of it. His portrait bronze is in the Prince of Wales Northern Heritage Centre."

"I was in Yellowknife airport talking to John Turner when he introduced me to **Robert Engle**. Engle was a former bush pilot who owned Northwest Territorial Airways. My nephew Reg, who flew me in his plane to many out-of-the-way settlements in the arctic to sculpt my portraits, was avidly interested in stories of the early bush pilots and their daring exploits, and he suggested I should sculpt the intrepid old flyer Ernie Boffa. I had already done Max Ward, and I was enthusiastic about doing more. I needed a commission. After a futile search among

Robert Engle OC, 1989

138

my affluent acquaintances, I wrote to Mr. Engle, and he showed considerable interest. He eventually gave me a commission to go to Los Angeles and sculpt Ernie's portrait.

"After the bust was cast in bronze, Mr. Engle presented it to the airport in Yellowknife. I was invited to the unveiling by Mr. Bernard Bouchard, the Minister of Transport. Mr. Engle asked me to do a portrait of his son, Jamie. As Mr. Engle had started out as a bush pilot, I felt that he should be amongst the others that I had done. I approached him and he agreed to sit for me, and invited me to stay with his family in their Yellowknife home. He also commissioned me to do a portrait of that much-decorated flyer, **C.E. (Punch) Dickins**. That bronze is in the aviation museum in Ottawa."

Ma Murray, Lillooet, BC, 1974

Other Portraits: Notable Subjects Around the World

Mrs. Murray was affectionately known as **Ma Murray**. She was a lovable, controversial, down-to-earth human being. Her editorials contained truths few writers would dare to print. She was blessed with a great sense of humour, and used her Irish wit frequently in her speech and writing. Her daughter, Georgina Keddle, wrote *The Newspapering Murrays*, about Ma and her husband, George Murray, MP.

"Ma posed for me in Lillooet in 1974, at her apartment above the printing plant. When I had completed the work, and after I had said goodbye to her, she called me back and, putting her hand in my breast pocket said, "I'm putting the fairies in your pocket and may they always bring you good luck." Then she drew my face down and kissed me. Ma passed away in 1982 at the age of ninety-five. She was awarded the Order of Canada in 1970.

"Another long distance head hunting expedition of mine was doing the bust of the great Russian pianist and conductor **Vladimir Ashkenazy**. I had never

Vladimir Ashkenazy,
celebrated pianist, Lausanne,
Switzerland, 1980

142

sculpted a musician of his stature. His 1980 Canadian concert tour was to take him to Montreal, Ottawa and Toronto. When he arrived in Montreal, I phoned him and he asked me to come to the Ritz Carlton Hotel as soon as possible. I was familiar with the layout of the lobby and rushed to the elevators. The one going up was crowded with a group of Brazilians but they motioned to me to enter. The doors closed and we slowly sank to the basement. In the crush, my head was alongside the emergency phone and I immediately advised the office of our predicament. They were aware of it and with great apologies said that it would be remedied in minutes! They didn't say how many! The lights were out and it was a bit frightening. There was much noisy chatter; however, because of our cramped quarters, the colourful Brazilian speech which is usually accompanied by much gesticulating had to be reduced to a minimum. My concern was about Ashkenazy, for he had said that he was pressed for time, and that he had a dinner engagement to attend.

"Finally, after almost twenty minutes, the doors were pried open and we moved into the basement. I rushed around looking for a staircase and bolted up to the third floor. On every floor a crowd was assembled waiting for the lift and Vladimir was waiting for me in the doorway of his suite. He explained that his hostess' chauffeur was down in the lobby and that I would have to meet him next morning at the Place des Arts at 11:00 AM, when he would be rehearsing. It was not a good start, and it proved to be an omen.

"I arrived at 10:45 and was ushered into the Green Room where I arranged my note book and callipers to record the major measurements of his face. One of the attendants nearby suggested that while waiting I should go into the concert hall. The rehearsal was going on and I sat in a box seat near a lady. I had never met Mrs. Ashkenazy but knew that she was of Icelandic parentage. We chatted and I showed her an album of photographs of my bronzes. She became quite excited when she saw a photo of a bronze which I had done of Ross Pratt and said that he had been her teacher when she was studying piano at the Royal Conservatory of Music in London.

"After the rehearsal, Ashkenazy joined me. We had hardly sat down before we were interrupted by an impresario, then the house manager and then a group of young people came in asking for his autograph. He was also called away for some international phone calls. However, between all these interruptions I was able to record most of his facial measurements.

"In two days' time, he was to play in Ottawa and 'maybe' he would be able to sit for me there. 'Maybe' turned out to be 'no' because of public and personal interviews and other business. He always travelled with his wife and youngest child and a nanny and tried to be with them as much as possible.

"His next concert was in Toronto and it was arranged that I meet him at the Park Plaza Hotel. We had one sitting which was interrupted by social phone calls. The story was repeated when I followed him to Tanglewood and then to New York. With profound apologies he informed me that the only time he could call his own was when he was at home on holidays. I asked him when he would be taking a holiday, and he said in mid-June. It happened that I expected to be doing some sculpting in Nyon, Switzerland about that time and I asked if it would be convenient for me to go to Lausanne then? I had sculpted two children's heads in Nyon but had not yet done the third child in the family. So the next year, upon returning to Switzerland, I went to Lausanne and finally finished his bust. This certainly was the longest head hunting experience of my sculpting life.

"Ashkenazy had three homes, one in Iceland, one in Greece and one in Lausanne. The latter was a very comfortable place set on a hill overlooking the city. Steps from the studio led down a graded garden at the rear. There was a large formal drawing room with a concert grand piano in it and a somewhat smaller music room with another grand piano in it, where he practised. Adjoining this was his study in which he had a large desk and walls shelved with his collection of records, tapes, musical manuscripts and photos of friends.

"He always posed for me sitting at his desk with a musical score propped up in front of him. My armature sat on the corner beside him. He always asked me to come at 11:00 AM, when he practised. Occasionally he would stop and listening carefully, he could hear his oldest son playing on the drawing-room piano and he would call out to him to play a certain Debussy étude for him. The lad was remarkably good at classical, boogie and rock!

"Ashkenazy practised for hours at a time, frequently the same three or four bars dozens of times, until it was perfect to his ears. I would sit there within sight of him, usually for about an hour, or until his wife or the housekeeper came in and announced that luncheon was served. He would leave the piano and come over and apologize and say, "We'll have a good session after lunch." This happened almost daily, yet he always asked me to come at eleven o'clock.

"Sitting at the table were his wife, the housekeeper-companion, a delightful English lady, the four children, Vladimir and myself. As an after-lunch ritual we all went for a walk in the garden. Then into the study. He would prop up a musical score and concentrate on it while I modelled his head. After studying the score for three quarters of an hour, he would fold it up and say, "Now I know it." I said, "How can you, you've not even touched a note?" and he said, "I just concentrate and it sinks in."

"Even at home, there were many interruptions. An agent or impresario might call regarding an upcoming recital in Asia or in America. How many minutes would the Beethoven Sonata No. 3 in A Flat Major take or perhaps the Brahms Sonata No. 3 in F Minor, opus 5. These are measured in minutes and seconds, as are the estimated time for applause, his backstage rest, reappearance to acknowledge the applause, second encore and maybe a third encore.

Schedules must be very carefully planned to allow him time to rest before rushing off to fulfil another engagement many miles or oceans away.

"If he was playing or conducting in any city within a reasonable distance of where I was, I always tried to attend, and always went backstage to receive a warm Russian bear hug from him. It was quite an education for me to learn a little of the personal life of a world famous artist.

"I am frequently asked who was the most interesting person ever to have posed for me. It might be **Mr. Chester Pickering**, a self-made industrialist. I like people who have been active and have done things with their lives.

"Mr. Pickering was a most outstanding individual, though he was basically quite humble, starting out by running away from home with ten cents in his pocket. When he was thirteen his mother died and his father remarried shortly after. He resented his stepmother's 'intrusion' and did not take kindly to her dictatorial ways. He left home shortly after and never returned.

"His life was a true Horatio Alger story. He ended up founding the Dustbane Company, which grew to be a thirty-five million dollar business, and the Lord Elgin Hotel in Ottawa. A book by Dean Walker entitled *Net Worth* tells the story of this outstanding individual.

"Although very wealthy, in his latter years he lived in a modest country house in Calabogie, Ontario. In winter, he went to Florida, not to a beautiful beach-front home or a sumptuous hotel, but to a comfortable, modest home. He had race horses and every day he went to the track. He told me, "I place a few bets and sometimes I make ten or fifteen bucks." This pleased him very much.

"Ashbury College and Carleton University in Ottawa were among the beneficiaries of his gen-erosity. He gave Carleton a substantial grant to bring guest lecturers to the uni-versity. The first in the series of lectures was given by an internationally-known professor from England

Chester Pickering,
industrialist, Ottawa, 1985

and his subject was sex. There wasn't an empty seat in the auditorium. On the platform were the president, the guest speaker and Mr. Pickering. The president spoke of Mr. Pickering's great interest in the university and his munificent financial assistance in providing for these lectures. He then asked Mr. Pickering to say a few words. Mr. Pickering was about ninety-five at that time, but never short on repartee, though his voice was a bit creaky. He stood up and graciously acknowledged the president's remarks but finished by saying "I don't know why the university spends so much money in bringing people from great distances to talk on sex. I've been married three times and I can tell you a few things about SEX!" The audience broke into laughter.

"Under much protest Mr. Pickering finally posed for his portrait bust in 1974. I went to his ninety-fifth birthday party when the bronze was officially unveiled and again went to his 100th birthday party. He passed away at 102 years of age. I am fortunate to have known such an outstanding man."

Herman Smith (Jackrabbit) Johannsen OC, Piedmont, Quebec, 1974

146

Born in Norway in 1875, **Herman Smith Johannsen** studied engineering in Berlin. He emigrated to the U.S.A. where he worked in his younger years and then moved to Canada in 1902. A great lover of the outdoors, he was an ardent cross-country skier and by his encouragement and example, induced hundreds of thousands of skiers, young and old, to pursue the sport. His name became a household word.

"It was Dr. Hans and Meg Weber who commissioned me to sculpt him. Jackrabbit posed for me at his home in Piedmont, Quebec when he was ninety-nine years old. When I stayed with him, he would retire about 9:30 PM and get up about 6:00 AM, dress in his ski clothes and ski on his private ski trail. Upon his return he would change his clothes and make breakfast for the two of us. He would not allow me in the kitchen. "No place for an artist." We would have a sitting, which was often interrupted by friendly neighbours who were curious to see me at work, or bringing in a casserole or some freshly baked muffins. He was much loved in the community and had wonderfully kind neighbours who kept an eye on him because he lived alone. Around 11:30, he would say, "It's about time we had a little sip, don't you think?" After a wee droppie, he would potter around the kitchen and prepare a meal for the both of us.

"I was amazed by his incredible memory; his stories were most instructive and entertaining. In the early thirties when he was laying out trails for developers at Lac Beauport, Mt. St. Castin, he spoke of having to get permission from the farmers and property owners to have the trails and the use of ski slopes on their property. They were all neighbours of ours, yet I could not recall half of their names. Our country home was at the opposite end of the lake where, in winter we frequently week-ended and skied.

"This delightful man was honoured by many sports organizations, and everyone was delighted when he was presented with the Order of Canada for his great contribution to sport. He passed away in Norway at the age of 111. Through the kindness of Dr. and Mrs. Weber, this bronze bust has been loaned to the Ski Museum in Ottawa."

Lotta Hitschmanova was one of a kind. She came to Canada as a refugee, and launched the Unitarian Service Committee of Canada (now USC Canada), with a dream of helping the thousands of children who were facing acute deprivation in a Europe devastated by World War II. All of her family except her sister had been exterminated in the Holocaust.

Her tireless efforts carried her work around the world, building USC Canada into a major agency that is a leader in international development, assisting people in over twenty countries. At the peak of her activities, she visited the Middle East, India, Bangladesh, Indonesia, South Korea and Southern Africa every year, inspecting USC projects, meeting with government leaders and local officials, working tirelessly for the welfare of the deprived wherever they were to be found. Many people will remember her radio talks describing the Unitarian Service Committee's work, ending with the familiar appeal to send a contribution to "USC, 56 Sparks Street, Ottawa."

Lotta Hitschmanova, Ottawa, 1970

147

"I sculpted Lotta's portrait in 1970. She was most reluctant to take the time for what she considered to be a vain project. She only had time to sit late at night, after her day's work was done, and she would turn up at about eleven o'clock, wearing her distinctive uniform, and I would give her a sandwich, for she seldom took the time to eat a proper meal during the day. She was a no-nonsense autocrat, in many ways, and she inspired great loyalty in those who worked with her. She passed away on August 1, 1990. Her bronze portrait bust is in the Unitarian Church in Ottawa.

"Since then I have sculpted a one-third-life-size high relief of her for the entrance to USC headquarters on Sparks Street in Ottawa."

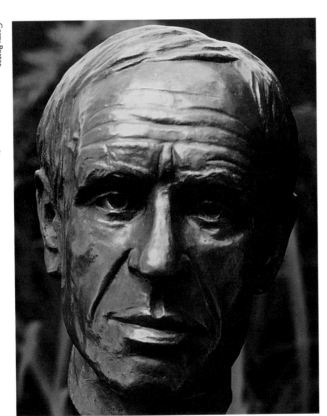

Gerry Porter

Douglas Cardinal, 1987

148

Born in Calgary in 1934, a student of architecture at the University of British Columbia, and a graduate of the University of Texas architecture programme, **Doug Cardinal** is Métis. He is now internationally admired and respected as an architect. Some of his best-known works are the Museum of Civilization in Hull Quebec, the Space and Science Centre in Edmonton, Alberta, St. Mary's Church in Red Deer, Alberta, and the National Museum of the American Indian, to be erected on The Mall in Washington, D.C. The flowing lines of his architecture have been described as "frozen music."

He says of himself, "I learned from my native ancestry the power of commitment and the magic of bringing something into being. I am involved in a dream in the making. It is a way for you to view yourself. That is what it is all about, dreams of what you could be. I went to the ceremonial lodge and I was given a vision. It is a vision of taking technology and creating something positive with it and maintaining my way of being in doing it. The Canadian Museum of Civilization is a true monument to our people."

Doug Cardinal sat for his portrait in Ottawa in 1987.

"**Prince Gatsha Buthelezi** was chief minister of the Kwazulus, and Minister of Home Affairs in the Mandela government. He sat for his portrait in Ulundi, Natal in 1984. Usually, a secretary called to tell me when he would be down for a sitting. On one particular day, I was expecting him at 2:15. I set up my armature and began checking the model with my measurements. I always record the principal facial measurements of my subjects at their first sitting, so that I can check the accuracy of my work as it progresses. I got quite a shock when I measured the flare of his nostrils; according to the chart they should have been half an inch wider! I was horrified that I could have made such an obvious error. Suddenly I realized that I had been looking at Bishop Tutu's measurements, which I had recorded on the other side of the same card!

Prince Gatsha Buthelezi, Natal, 1984

"I was chuckling to myself when the prince came in, and he asked me why I had the cheshire cat grin. I had not told him that I was also sculpting the bishop, and we both had a good laugh about my error.

"As a sculptor, and one of perhaps a handful of whites in Ulundi, I was quite a novelty. The staff of the Holiday Inn were intrigued by what was taking place in my room. I was visited by Bishop Alpheus Zulu, the Speaker of the House, and some of the councillors, and the prince's family. They were shy about offering comment even when I pressed them.

"His mother Princess Magoogoo, a charming little lady, was very musical, and collected folk songs and recorded the music of the Zulus. My work there was a delightful experience, and my empathy with the prince was more than cordial. He was demonstrative and affectionate, and we discovered among our many common interests a love for classical and liturgical music.

"The bust was commissioned by Mr. Harry Oppenheimer, the great South African industrialist. The bronze was cast at a foundry in Pretoria and presented to the National Assembly in Ulundi, Natal, South Africa.

149

Harold Pfeiffer with portrait painted by Vladimir Praskov during his visit to Siberia in 1988

The Man Who Makes Heads With his Hands

arold Pfeiffer's retirement from the National Museum freed him to pursue his head hunting as much as commissions and his own inclinations allowed. In the decade of the seventies, he completed 107 sculptures. A look at the list of his works in Appendix II reveals a steady flow of portrait commissions interspersed with concentrated bursts of aboriginal and arctic subjects.

This was a time for Harold to enjoy his freedom to travel and exercise his creative gifts. In 1974 he logged 34,000 air miles, making several trips to northern Europe and Greenland. In his Christmas letter for 1978 he writes of a cruise in the Caribbean, a major solo show in Toronto (*The Survivors*, The Gallery, First Canadian Place), an arctic sculpting tour that took in Inuvik, Fort Norman and Hay River, on to Edmonton, where he sculpted Ralph Steinhauer, the Lieutenant-Governor of Alberta, then his Max Ward portrait adventure, a visit to Leo Mol in Winnipeg, and three weeks in Bermuda, giving illustrated talks on his work and on people of the arctic while executing yet another portrait, of the shipping magnate Charles Tregenza, and all without anything like a fortune of his own to finance it. Harold Pfeiffer is not a wealthy man. Every leg of the journey represents measureless efforts at letter-writing, telephone calls, buttonholing prospects at parties, following up conversations remembered from years before, inviting yet another new friend to come to his home and look at his work, and digging up business cards pocketed at this opening or that reception at any time in the previous ten years.

Throughout his career, Harold Pfeiffer has had to rely on his own initiative to generate work. Commissions rarely came easily. Sometimes he would execute a portrait and find buyers afterwards, which was a gamble for someone with very little money of his own. His self-confessed proclivity for name-dropping and his gregarious nature kept him in contact with a world of potential patrons. In a typical chain of events, a chance encounter in the Museum of Fine Arts in Montreal led to a friendship with Jan Berglund, a Swedish diplomat. Berglund was posted on to Peru, and eventually returned to Sweden for military service, and left the diplomatic service. They kept in touch, and when Harold was stymied on a trip to Munich when the friend he intended to visit suffered a serious accident, he altered his plans and went to visit Jan in Sweden instead. He was surprised to find him living in the family's fifty-four-room castle, and had a very pleasant stay, in spite of there being only one bathroom, and their friendship was renewed. Jan subsequently moved on to Switzerland, and when Harold visited him there in 1978, he had him show photos of his work to an artist he knew, who remarked, "You should be doing some work here. Start tomorrow!" Harold replied that he was ready whenever a commission could be found. He was soon engaged to go to Nyon to do portraits of the three children of Sven Eric Persson, a wealthy Swedish businessman. He completed two that year and the following year completed the third, and took the opportunity to visit Vladimir Ashkenazy and complete that portrait as well, which he was doing on his own without a commission. Because of this knack of fostering aquaintanceships so that they grow into friendships, Harold Pfeiffer managed to create a network of private supporters who made his unique career possible.

Because his career spans a time in which classical realism, representational art, has been out of fashion in the art world, serious critical commentary on Harold Pfeiffer's work is hard to find in print. Most of the voluminous press coverage of his exhibitions and sculpting activities is largely uncritical descriptive reportage, though occasionally an art journalist's opinion can be found:

His work is realistic in the best sense of the word. The strength of the native and the forceful character of the famous or the delicate beauty of the very young, all emerge with equal clarity from the formless clay under his hands. (Karl Weiselberg, Ottawa *Citizen*)

He is a portrait sculptor who has sensitively interpreted a profound feeling for humanity and a considerable degree of aesthetic value in his sculptured heads. (Andrei Zodorozny, Montreal *Gazette*)

The Toronto Star published an article on February 4, 1979, "Ottawa Sculptor Chipping Away at Art Policies—Why Is the Art Establishment Ignoring Harold Pfeiffer?" by Sol Littman, which tackles the conundrum rather inconclusively.

However, his achievements have not gone entirely unrecognised. His work has been shown at numerous Canadian and American exhibitions (see Appendix III), and at two of the world's great galleries: the Royal Academy and the National Portrait Gallery in London, England. Guest books from his shows are filled with thousands of accolades and expressions of gratitude. Pfeiffer's sculpture can be fairly compared to the work of Catlin, Curtis, Krieghoff and Remington, whose paintings, photographs and sculptures are continually studied by anthropologists and students of the sociology of nineteenth-century life.

There is no shortage of very positive commentary about its historical and social significance:

Pfeiffer is the only artist in the world who has diligently and artistically recorded likenesses of native people, a heritage for all time...Pfeiffer's collection is a national historical heritage and... it should upon no account be separated. It is a national treasure.
(Dr. James Cruise, former director of the Royal Ontario Museum)

Pfeiffer deserves the gratitude of every Canadian. Without men of his devotion and extraordinary perception, an entire civilization might have passed away without leaving a trace of its going. His splendid portraits in bronze will live on forever.
(Honourable Mr. Justice Thomas Berger)

Mr. Pfeiffer's works depict the dignity and strength, as well as the sorrows and endurance, of elders, artists and community leaders of peoples who have been determined to survive and flourish in the face of great odds.
(Rosemarie Kuptana, President, Inuit Tapirisat)

Harold Pfeiffer is not a grandly expressive man. He will not analyzes his own work, and describes his subjects in simple direct terms. When pressed, he will point to his sculpture and say, "This is what I saw; this is who she was." What crops up most consistently is his appreciation of subjects who are, in his favourite word, real. Again and again, going over the tales of his life, his comments return to this theme: "There was nothing phony about her...he was a down-to-earth character...she looked me in the eye and always said what she thought...he was one of the real ones...they were great people." These evaluations transcend any kind of cultural bias or partisanship; he found Bishop Desmond Tutu somewhat arrogant and standoffish, while Prince Gatsha Buthelezi impressed him with his warmth and expressive affection.

A good portrait is more than a physical likeness. It is a recognition on the part of the artist of the character of the sitter. Harold Pfeiffer is a sympathetic portraitist, and his best work shows his admiration for his subjects. His preference for mature subjects is a leaning towards the clear revelation of character in the lines of the face. His Kenojuak and Elizapee, One Gun and Annie Waterlilypad, Marius Barbeau and Georges Vanier show a masterful balancing of the objectifying eye of an artist, observing the subject as an object of light, shadow, masses, lines and planes, and the empathetic eye of a friend, recognising the integrity of a fellow human being.

"Putting my thoughts down about sculpture and sculpting is most difficult. I can't say more than that my large harvest of bronze portraits is an honest concrete story of my first love, sculpting. I have tried to convey to the viewer a true likeness of the subject. There is more to likeness than the simple dimension of facial features which, of course, I respect. Karsh understood this and achieved his famous photograph of an aroused and indomitable war-time leader by suddenly snatching away Winston Churchill's cigar. The sculptor neither needs nor can use such tricks. The modelling process of sculpting takes time, and a relationship develops which, consciously or not, affects the way the sculptor sees his subject.

"It is hard to explain. There is a story that Abraham Lincoln refused to make a political appointment proposed by his staff, saying, to their astonishment, that he did not like his looks. He explained that while appearance may or may not be only skin deep, 'in my view a man over forty is responsible for his own face.' It is something like that that has kept my focus on realistic portrait sculpture even though the main currents of our age are still overwhelmingly towards abstract art.

The aboriginal portraits are an irreplaceable record of a vanished people. These are the ones who lived in the land before their way of life was completely shattered by the arrival of Europeans; they have their vigorous lives and indomitable spirit etched on their faces. The irreversible changes that have taken place in their way of life mean that faces like these will never be seen again. They represent a heritage for Canada's aboriginal peoples, and for all of us, that is valuable beyond price. They are a vivid reminder that all human societies were founded by survivors like these.

"I was uniquely privileged to be able to work so extensively in the north among Canada's native peoples, and to be able to search out and sculpt men and women who had grown up and raised their families in a harsh world still scarcely touched by modern civilization. What people, and what faces!"

Harold with Kenojuak at her retrospective exhibition at the McMichael Gallery, 1986

Appendix I: Sculpting, from Model to Bronze Cast

The process begins with modelling. The sculptor sets up an armature, a mount for the clay model, with some provision for turning it so that the sculptor can work on it from all sides without having to get up and move around. The modelling is done in plasticine, which holds its shape but remains plastic for a long time without needing to be kept damp as clay does, so that it can be worked and reworked until the likeness is satisfactory. To save weight, a styrofoam wig mount can form the core of the model, if a human head is the subject.

When the model has been successfully completed, a mould must be made for casting. Sometimes the foundry will make a rubber negative mould from the plasticine model, but usually the sculptor will make a plaster cast which is more stable and easily protected from damage during handling. Harold makes a plaster waste mould by flicking freshly mixed plaster on the original with his fingers until a layer of sufficient depth has been built up, about 1/2″. He separates the two halves, and removes the plasticine, so that a perfect negative in plaster is left. He cleans the two plaster shells thoroughly, ties them together and pours in freshly mixed plaster after coating the interior with soapy water or glycerine. The plaster is poured very carefully to ensure no air bubbles are formed.

A first coating of plaster, to a depth of about 1/4″ is tinted with ochre or blueing. This is very important because it makes the boundary between the negative mould and the positive mould, the model, very clear. The second coating covers the interior surfaces of the mould to a depth of about 1/2″. This makes a hollow casting, which is much lighter than a solid casting would be. The moulds are chipped off with a blunt chisel when the new plaster has set, leaving a perfect replica of the original model, in plaster. The tinting of the first layer becomes important here, in helping ensure that all the plaster from the mould is removed, and none of the plaster from the model. When it is thoroughly dry, Harold gives it a coat of shellac to seal it. "This last stage, removing the waste mould, is one of the most exciting pleasures of sculpting."

At the foundry, the plaster model is covered with a layer a centimetre or more thick of one of a number of rubber compounds which pick up all the fine detail. A plaster mould, called a mother mould, is poured around the rubber to provide support. When the rubber is peeled off in two halves and set in its plaster supports, it is used to make a wax mould that exactly matches the original model in all details. The wax is poured in and swished around to build up a layer as thick as the final bronze cast is to be. The resulting hollow wax model is carefully cleaned up and wax rods are attached that lead to a central point or cup at the top. The model is coated and filled with refractory material to make the foundry mould. The whole is fired in a kiln, which melts the wax out as it bakes the refractory material, creating the ceramic shell mould into which the molten bronze is poured.

When the bronze has cooled, the ceramic shell is broken and sand-blasted away, and the rods or sprues are cut off. The bronze can then be patinated; left to itself, bronze gradually acquires a patina caused by the oxidation of its surface. Most bronze sculptures are painted with reagent chemicals to simulate this effect immediately. Bronze is about ninety percent copper, combined with silicone, tin, manganese, zinc and other metals in various proportions. Older bronzes have more tin, modern bronzes are usually silicone bronzes. The bronze can be darkened with sulphur compounds which react with the copper. Various nitrates, chlorides and acetates may be brushed on to give overtones from green to blue. A little burnishing will relieve the patina in highlighted spots, and an application of paste wax will preserve the desired appearance. A clear plastic coating is even more durable.

There are other ways of simulating the patina of age. The late Count Eigel Knuth, a distinguished Danish archaeologist and sculptor, had an unusual way of creating patina on his works. He used urine, which is an excellent reagent that creates a very natural patina on bronze. Harold met him while he was on the staff of the National Museum in Ottawa, and Knuth was visiting, doing some research there. His main field of work was Greenland, and he had sculpted portraits of Greenlanders in bronze and stone, which gave them something important in common. On two occasions, among his many trips to Denmark, Harold visited Eigel in his fifth floor apartment with a number of other guests, and the beverage served was beer. At the end of the evening, the guests were escorted down to the garden, where Eigel had an assortment of his bronzes assembled for the "Patination Ritual," and everyone urinated on his art.

"Probably my greatest worry was when my modelling was finished and I was about to make the moulds and the plaster cast. Casting is an art in itself. In the studio at home, there is plenty of hot and cold running water, a large washbasin full of water in which to quickly wash mixing bowls, spoons or spatulas as one is mixing or pouring the creamlike plaster of Paris into the mould. It all has to be done just at the right time. You have to do it yourself; you know the right consistency; there is really no one whom you can absolutely trust to do the things you want done at the exact moment. In the arctic, conditions were not so ideal. The language barrier is always there and anyway, at home there are bags of plaster of Paris, separation fluid, globs of plasticine at hand to prop up a corner which might not be level or some hole which must be filled in a moment's notice. There is a pot on the bench filled with a variety of brushes, just the right one to dust some loose bit of hard plaster which managed to get into the mould. There is probably a chum alongside who has assisted you on some previous casting job. You can shout at him, "Get this! Hand me that! Hold this while I get some more plaster! Quick, mix a small bowl of plaster and use very hot water, that will make it set sooner and it will marry better with the rest of the plaster! Give me the rubber spatula, quick. Hold this end." And so on. It can be nerve-wracking! Once the plaster has set, that is it. It cannot be reworked.

"It was a rare occasion when I ever had anyone helping me do my casting in the arctic. It is a very important procedure and I usually did it at a time when I knew that I would not have any young visitors who might take it into their heads to start a rough house and accidently bump into me at a critical moment. I am usually quite nervous when I make moulds and do not like any distractions while at work.

"This day I had gathered everything together, plenty of water, mixing bowls, wooden spoons, spatula, brushes, and all. The two moulds were all washed out and tied together for the plaster to be poured into them. The interiors were damp so that the new plaster would not be absorbed into the mould too fast leaving the surface crumbly. I mixed the plaster and was gently stirring when I realized that I had not brushed on the glycerine that prevents the new plaster sticking to the old plaster. I rushed over to the window sill where I always kept the glycerine; it was missing. Someone had lifted it. Thinking fast, I opened three or four cans of sardines in the kitchen and poured all the oil into a bowl. There was precious little but I hurriedly brushed the interior of the mould with what I had. It was quite an exercise getting my hand and brush through the neck into the mould. My precious plaster was ready to pour and I sloshed it into the mould just before it set on me. Glycerine or soapy water have body and leave just sufficient separation to prevent new plaster sticking to the old plaster without altering any of the detail. My only hope was that the sardine oil would do the same job. When properly set, moulds usually can be chipped off very easily, but in this case, it was only in a few areas where the mould loosened without problems.I finally had to chip it all off very gingerly. The result was more or less recognisable as a head with the main features but certainly not the man who had originally posed for me. Of course I had to redo it, and had him sit for me again. He did not object because he knew that I would pay him again for his time. Upon my return south, a man was particularly taken by the first effort and purchased it. It really did not resemble my work very much and later I learned that he had put it up for auction in Montreal and that it sold for a much greater amount than he had paid for it. Maybe I should smudge more of my work!

"I have always paid particular attention to the sitter's eyes, for they are the first thing which one looks at; they are the soul of the person. Catching light and shade in sculpture is of first importance. I have received many compliments for the way I portray a person's eyes. The colour is governed by the depth of the depression of the pupil; for a person who has pale blue eyes, the depression is very slight, whereas for someone with very dark eyes, a more profound depression is required. These little tricks bring life into the eye."

Appendix II: Sculptures by Harold Pfeiffer

1933   Don Ashmun
        Thomas Muldrup Forsythe

1934   Mother
        Lois Reynolds Kerr

1935   Stannye Musson
        Captain Joseph Bernier

1936   Jaqueline Darveau

1938   Wolf Cub
        George Mitchell Mitchell
        Dalila Barbeau

1939   Helen Irving Cook
        Alphonse de Grandmaison
        C. Anthony Law
        Joseph Bouchard
        Ross Pratt
        Arthur Leblanc
        Luc Lacourciere CC
        Colonel Walter Ray

1940   Mark Pfeiffer
        John Agnes
        Hon. Charlach Mackintosh
        Peter & Pamela, War Guests
        Richard Shand

1941   Shirley Ross Goldsmith
        Peggy McKay, War Worker

1942   Mrs. Lees Playfair Reazin
        Gray Wilson

1943   Sir Robert Borden
        Leo Ciceri

1944   Teja Singh
        Taiwo Solarin
        Lord Donald Ogden
        Alistair de Tessier Prevost
        Portia White
        David Ojo Abiodun Oguntoye

1945   Colonel Patrick Baird

1946   Jack Fenwick
        Miss Marion Scott

1947   Ardra Pfeiffer Fradinger
        Shu Feng Ch'eh
        Judy Holbrooke
        Iain Scherbeck
        William Primrose

1948   Mel Macdonald
        Joel Trosch
        Billy Mennen
        Esther Glatt
        Janet Horne
        Martha Farnsworth
        Judy (Oona) Friday
        Jack Howard

1949   Yousuf Karsh
        Jean Pierre Maltais
        Mrs. Erskine Buchanan

1950   John Udd
        Mary Udd
        Richard Udd

1951	Desmond MacDiarmid
	Ballet dancers (plaques)
	Indian trapper's homestead (relief)
1952	Bill McCrudden
	Tom Bishop
	Floral panels (reliefs)
	Fruit panels (reliefs)
1953	May Willmot
	Lap Herder
	Family crests (3)
1954	Illya
	Tommy Palliser
	Lothar Schaeffer
	Elizabee
	Old Willya
	Alicee (mask)
	Charles Blau
	Tye
	Waino Aaltonen
1955	Normie Kwong
	Dr. Thomas O'Hagan
	Black Sleep
	David Komoyuk
1956	Paul Green
	Janet Green
	Josee (Warming Hands)
	Ooah
	Pootoogak
1957	Martha Simonee & Baby
	Janet Turnbull
	Kibbewe Ashagrie
1958	Dr. Marius Barbeau

1959	Dr. Alan Crockford
	Adamie Kalingo
1960	Al Porter
	Stevenson Gardner
	Sarah Bradford,
	Viscountess Bangor
	Jill Walker
	Susan Walker
1961	Low Reliefs
1962	Margo Willmot
	Julie Willmot
1963	Old Mischief
	Seagull
	Puffins
	Owls
	Gyrfalcon
1964	Jody Sullivan
	Janet Sullivan (relief)
1965	Mimi Sullivan
	Jeff Nicholson
	Gordon Burrows
1966	Alma Houston
	Dr. Andrew Stewart
	Dr. Zeph. Rousseau
1967	Governor-General Georges Vanier
	Linda Gerstley
	Jimmy Gerstley
	Nancy Anderson
	Matthew Kumashie
	Jill Oppenheimer
	Joann Oppenheimer
	Paul Oppenheimer

Mary Reeves
Dr. Harold Geggie
Hon. H. W. Herridge, MP

1968 Kenojuak CC, RCA
Stephen Angulalik
Michael Kangoak
"Old Bill" Oshooknoak
Patrick Koagatark
Satkatsiak
Zacharie Itimangak
Theresa Kernak
Kingmitiak
Okpik
Jacob Sassinak-Kringorn
Helena Karmatsiak
Nigel Wilford
Hugh Wilson

1969 Roloff Beny OC
Vreni Winser
Chief Dan George OC
Elizapee Padlayat
Mrs. Patrick Coulson

1970 Dr. Wallace Shute
Dr. Lotta Hitschmanova CC
Senator Donald Cameron
Esther Fine
Frank Clair

1971 Robert Sexton
Charles Sexton
Jamie Bowden
Charles Mussen
Rebesca
Peter Baker
John Goodall
Alexis Charlo
Teddy Collie
Chief Jimmy Bruneau
Mahik

1972 Philippa Harris
Dr. George Gooderham
Mrs. Martha Cohen OC
Abebba Hyenda
Chief Julien Yendo
Chief John Lamalice
Tom Dornboss
Rev. Father Vandevelde, OMI
Maurice Curliss
Johnny Powderface
Dick Starlight
Chief Joe Crowfoot
Chief David Crowchild
Chief Jim Shot-Both-Sides
Chief Ben Calfrobe
Chief John Sampson
Chief Frank Kaquitts
One Gun
Willie Scraping White
Earl Calfchild
Mrs. James Gladstone
Tom Kaquitts

1973 Mrs. Donald Early
Bent J. Sivertz
Hugh Keenleyside CC
Major General Hugh Young
Albert Faille
Air Marshall Hugh Campbell
Rev. Pierre Henry OMI
Commissioner S.M. Hodgson CC
Annie (Macpherson) Waterlilypad
Mrs. Salteau LeNoir
Christopher Weber
Hon. Gordon Robertson PC

1974 George Washington Porter
Helen Kalvak CC, RCA
Ikey Bolt
Pernille Zeltner
Margaret "Ma" Murray
Rev. Brother Jaques Volant OMI

165

Herman Smith-Johannsen OC
John Odams
The Cadet
Robert Bell Douglas

1975 Elizabeth Jensen
Lars Rasmussen
Hosias Carlsen
Isaak Carlsen
Judithe Henrikson
Apollus Noahsen
Vittus Jorgensen
Bjorn Egethe
Simon Petrussen
Annikatrina Josefsen
J. Gordon Gibson
Mary-Ellen Burns

1976 Mabel Steffanson
Deputy Commissioner
    John Parker CC
Chief Johnny Kay
Chief Johnny Tetlichi
Kenneth Peeloolook
Lorenz Learmonth
Jimmy Holyoke
Mrs. Ron (Bunny) Charlton
The Welcomers

1977 Gina Leibrecht
Hon. Mr. Justice
    Thomas Berger
HM Queen Elizabeth II
Samantha Wood
Commissoner L. Nicholson OC
Gus D'Aoust
Maxwell Ward
Charlotte Zeltner
Penelope Zeltner
Pernilla Zeltner

Kaspar Klitgaard
Captain Viktor Pelezj

1978 Kitty Rolland
Annie Novalinga
Philapusie Novalinga
Father L. Ducharme OMI
Mans Persson
Melin Persson

1979 Thomas Zeltner
Harriet Gladue
Harry Camsell
Paula Cowpland
Christine Cowpland
Marcus Leibrecht
Charles Tregenza
Mrs. Ellen Burns
Mons Persson

1980 Lt. Governor
    Ralph Steinhauer OC
Mario Bottazinni
Hon. Mr. Justice
    Angelo Branca
Vladimir Ashkenazy
Paul Kaeser
Father G-M Rosseliere OMI
Terracotta masks (9)

1981 Sandy MacTaggart
Count Jean de la Bruyére
Gus Kraus
Mary Kraus
Jennefer Kraus
Eve Osler Hampson
Terracotta masks (11)

1982 Andrew Slipchenko
William Heeney

Mike Patterson
Terry Fox
Dr. Sun Yat Sen
Terracotta masks (7)

1983 Captain Daniel Danielsen
Leigh Berry
Senator Thérèse Casgrain CC
Nicholas de Janitsary
Terracotta masks (8)

1984 Prince Gatsha Buthelezi
Archbishop Desmond Tutu
Peter Baker
John Hazen
Montague Aldous
Bernie Will Brown

1985 Captain Telesfor Bielicz
Madeline Gyurkovich
Steve Fonyo
Chester Pickering

1986 Lester B. Pearson
Yuri Khromykn

1987 Douglas Cardinal OC
Douglas Pfeiffer
Ernie Boffa
Grey Nun

1988 George MacDonald
Frogs
Nuns
Mikhail Gorbachev
Ayaya Tagyok
Galena Ataquay
Josef Inmauge
Yuri Pukalik

Dr. Vladimir Koravye
Tatooed Woman of
  Chokotka
Praxmyre Rakhtunie
Vasily Emrykaya

1989 Robert P. Engle
Mrs. Jean Davis
Brook Wessle

1990 C.E. (Punch) Dickins

1992 Dr. Wilbert Keon OC
Richard Weber
Dr. Bruce Baker
Peter Duncan
Darden Coors

1993 Noona
Small masks and reliefs
Three Inuit Boys (high relief)

1994 Mother & Child (relief)
Lotta Hitschmanova (miniature)
Black Sleep (reduction)
Annie Waterlilypad (reduction)

1996 Rodolfo Goetz-Blohm
Heidi Homes
Captain Jens Thorne

Appendix III: Exhibitions and Collections

Group Exhibitions

Cowansville Art Centre, Cowansville, Quebec

Hamilton Art Gallery, Hamilton, Ontario

London Art Gallery, London, Ontario

Montreal Museum of Fine Art, Spring Shows, Montreal, Quebec

National Council of Jewish Women, Ottawa, Ontario

National Portrait Gallery, London, England

Ontario Society of Artists, Toronto, Ontario

Royal Academy, London, England

Royal Canadian Academy, Montreal, Quebec & Toronto, Ontario

Sculptors' Society of Canada, Montreal, Quebec & Toronto, Ontario

Spring Festival Louisville, Kentucky

Western Ontario Exhibition, London, Ontario

Wilstead Art Gallery, Windsor, Ontario

Solo Exhibitions

Allied Art Centre, Calgary, Alberta

Beckett Gallery, Hamilton, Ontario

Brock University, St. Catharines, Ontario

Calgary Galleries, Calgary Alberta

Canadian Embassy, Washington, D.C.

Centennial Gallery, The Citadel, Halifax, Nova Scotia

Château Frontenac, Quebec City, Quebec

Department of External Affairs, Ottawa, Ontario

F.J. Cooper Gallery, Philadelphia, Pennsylvania

First Canadian Place, Toronto, Ontario

Gustave Gallery, Niagara-on-the-Lake, Ontario

Inauguration of Arctic Council, Canadian Museum of Civilization

Keenleyside Gallery, Vancouver, BC

King Ranch Health Spa, King City, Ontario

King Ranch Health Spa, King City, Ontario

Lefévre Gallery, Edmonton, Alberta

Lester B. Pearson Building, Ottawa, Ontario

Lethbridge University, Lethbridge, Alberta

MacDowell Gallery, Toronto, Ontario

Mandel Gallery, Saskatoon, Saskatchewan

Montreal Museum of Fine Arts, Montreal, Quebec

Mount Allison University, Sackville, New Brunswick

Mount Royal College, Calgary, Alberta

Organisation of American States, Washington, D.C.

"First Art Exhibition in the Arctic" Pelly Bay, Northwest Territories

Provincial Museum, Edmonton, Alberta

Roberts Gallery, Toronto, Ontario

Robertson Gallery, Ottawa, Ontario

Royal Ontario Museum, Toronto, Ontario

St. Foy Municipal Gallery, Quebec City, Quebec

Sullivan Gallery, Huntington Valley, Pennsylvania

Terasse de la Chaudiere, Hull, Quebec

University of Ottawa, Ottawa, Ontario

Wells Gallery, Ottawa, Ontario

WHAS Gallery, Louisville, Kentucky

Public Collections

Alberta House, London, England

Brock University, St. Catharines, Ontario

Canadian Cancer Society Headquarters, Toronto, Ontario

Churchill Museum, Churchill, Manitoba

City of Ottawa, Ottawa, Ontario

Glenbow Museum, Calgary, Alberta

J.B. Speed Museum, Louisville, Kentucky

La Musée d'art de Joliette, Joliette, Quebec

Museum of Civilization, Hull, Quebec

Prince of Wales Northern Heritage Centre, Yellowknife, Northwest Territories

R.C.M.P. Museum, Regina, Saskatchewan

Sculptors' Society of Canada, Permanent Collection, Toronto, Ontario

Public Monuments

Dr. Thomas O'Hagan, Jasper, Alberta

Dr. H.J.G. Geggie, Wakefield, Quebec

Lotta Hitschmanova, USC Building, Ottawa, Ontario

Lotta Hitschmanova, Unitarian Church, Ottawa, Ontario

Prince Gatsha Buthelezi, Ulundi, KwaZulu, South Africa

Private Collections

R. Angus Corporation, Edmonton, Alberta

Harry Keller Collection, Lausanne, Switzerland

Per Klitgaard Collection, Nuuk, Greenland

Ambassador Ulf Lewin Collection, Stockholm, Sweden

Henry Moore Collection, Much Badham, England

Sven Eric Persson Collection, Nyon, Switzerland

Mogens V. Zeltner Collection, UggelØse, Denmark

Index of Proper Names

About the Authors

John Stevens is a writer and editor with a special interest in the stories of unsung heroes. He has written and edited numerous works of fiction and nonfiction, including *Encounters: Early Images of Canada's Aboriginal Peoples* (General Store Publishing House, 1996). He lives in Toronto and Outram, Nova Scotia.

Portrait of Harold Pfeiffer by Ottawa sculptor Meg Weber-Crockford

Harold Pfeiffer's work has been exhibited in Canada, the United States and England, and is held in two major museum collections in Canada and in numerous private collections around the world. He is the only sculptor to complete a collection of bronze portraits of the circumpolar people. He lives in Ottawa.

177

Sadly, Harold passed away April 12, 1997, as this book was being prepared for publication. He remained actively involved until a few weeks before his death and was eagerly looking forward to finally seeing his story in print.

For more copies of:

THE MAN WHO MAKES HEADS WITH HIS HANDS
The Art and Life of Harold Pfeiffer, Sculptor

For hard cover copy send $49.95 plus $6.00 GST, shipping and handling
For soft cover copy send $29.95 plus $5.00 GST, shipping and handling to:
General Store Publishing House
1 Main Street, Burnstown
Ontario, Canada K0J 1G0
(613) 432-7697 or 1-800-465-6072

Also

ENCOUNTERS
Early Images of Canada's Aboriginal Peoples
From the Library Collections of the Geological Survey of Canada

send $18.95 plus $4.50 for GST, shipping and handling to:
General Store Publishing House
1 Main Street, Burnstown
Ontario, Canada K0J 1G0
(613) 432-7697 or 1-800-465-6072